WHAT OTHERS ARE SAYING

CU00730541

I love this book! It holds the keys nee From extensive research, Stuart Robinson paints a broad sweep across the canvas of time and fills it with exhilarating stories of victories won when people pray. He also gives sobering warnings of advances made by the kingdom of darkness when we the ecclesia do not follow the words of Christ "My house shall be called a house of prayer."

As the author has written, history shows that there is seldom a record of a prayerless revival. This book will bring you to your knees.

Jennifer Hagger AM
Founder and Former Director, Australian House of Prayer for All Nations and Mission World Aid, South Pacific Coordinator for The Global Watch, Australia

Prayer Power – Changing the World and You is a must read for all intercessors or people who wish to understand and explore in a deeper way how prayer can impact individual lives and the situations we face every day in our world. An easy-to-read book that is well researched and liberally sprinkled with stories which bring the power and experience of prayer to life. After reading it you will want to pray and test out this powerful tool that God has given us to change the circumstances of your life. If ever you doubted the power of prayer this book will convince you of its reality.

Brian Pickering
National Coordinator, Australian Prayer Network

In a post-COVID-19 season of fear, suspicion and uncertainty, the least we can do is often the most we can do: PRAY – or, as Stuart Robinson so eloquently defines it, "Deploy our Spiritual power."

Prayer Power – Changing the World and You contains invaluable, practical guidelines that will equip the reader for a life of prayer. What makes this book unique is that not only does it provide practical principles to edify the reader into a life of communion but it also provides amply illustrations that will encourage the reader to a life of influence

Prayer, as someone once said, is not only there as a spare wheel, but as a steering wheel – not only for emergencies and release, but as a daily discipline and a sustaining power in times of need. This is what this book is all about: Read it, live it and experience it!

Mike Burnard

Former Vice-President, Open Doors International and Founder of INcontext International. Currently serving as Analytical Strategist at dia-LOGOS, South Africa.

Prayer Power – Changing the World and You is the best book I have read so far about prayer and its powerful effects. It covers so many important aspects of prayer. It is convincing and challenging. It will change your life. It is an urgent and most necessary call to Christians around the world to dedicate themselves to fervent persistent prayer. If we need anything today, it is a reversal of the rapid spiritual decline of many churches and countries. To see changes we need to follow the example of the Godly men and women mentioned in this book. They experienced great revivals, saw God's power to change the lives of multitudes of people, societies, governments and the course of history in nations.

The ministry of Shelter Now International among the nations has always been strongly based on prayer. Stuart's book has challenged me not only to keep our commitment to prayer but to deepen it.

Georg Taubmann

International Director, Shelter Now International, Germany

Having been involved in the movement of prayer nationally and internationally for nearly 40 years, I was curious to find out what more I could gain in reading another book on prayer.

Stuart Robinson answered my curiosity in a powerful way by reminding me that prayer is more about fellowship and communion with an Omnipotent, Omniscient, and Omnipresent Triune God than it is about me and my needs.

Having said that, I found *Prayer Power – Changing the World and You* refreshing, stimulating, faith building and at times deeply challenging. I know it will do the same for you. I would strongly recommend anyone who longs for a deeper sense of God's presence in their lives, in their church and in their communities to read it carefully and prayerfully.

Ian Cole
Founder, World Prayer Centre, England

Stuart Robinson has written a book on prayer called *Prayer Power – Changing the World and You*. You may have an impression of what a book on prayer would be like. I am convinced that this book will be completely unexpected.

Prayer Power – Changing the World and You is a tour de force across history, the globe, the Bible and the author's personal experiences that will challenge your prayer life. If this book does not drive you to prayer, it can only be because you did not read it thoroughly. Many pray out of duty or desperation. This book will drive you to prayer through passion and inspiration. It is my hope that many will read this book and it will revolutionize our prayer and revitalize our faith.

Karl Faase
CEO, Olive Tree Media, Australia

Stuart Robinson's new book *Prayer Power – Changing the World and You* is full to the brim with culturally diverse, divinely inspired and spiritually authentic examples of God at work—both today and as He has been—throughout history. It's full of inspiring biblical examples and exhortations that point us to an ever-closer relationship with a loving Father in heaven. An inspiring read for any and all who wish to have a closer relationship with Him, hear His voice, do what He says and help advance His kingdom on earth. May it also help us to move the mountains in our lives and around us and prepare for the coming Revival.

Brian Mills

*Founder, Interprayer International Partnership,
Senior Advisor of the International Prayer Council,
Member of the International Reconciliation Coalition, England*

Another book on prayer? No! It is about the Power of Prayer, the explosive Power which demands our utmost efforts to experience it. Those breath-taking witnesses described in this book inspired me and at the same time humbled me, as if I heard Jesus speaking to me: "Until now you have not asked for anything in my name. Ask and you will receive and your joy will be complete" (John 16:24). This book helps me understand what "the complete joy" is about: fully experiencing the explosive and life changing Power of Prayer that is changing the lives of my family.

Dr Liu Xuanqing
Pastor, Shanghai Church, China

PRAYER POWER

Changing the World and You

by

Stuart Robinson

Award Winning & Best Selling Author

BY THE SAME AUTHOR

Mosques & Miracles: Revealing Islam and God's Grace

Defying Death: Zakaria Botross – Apostle to Islam

Traveling Through Troubled Times

The Prayer of Obedience (Revised 2016)

The Promise of Vision

The Challenge of Islam

Islam Rising – The Middle East and Us

The Hidden Half – Women and Islam

Daring To Disciple – Making Jesus' Last Command Our First Priority

Persevering Prayer – Growing Your Church Supernaturally

Positioning For Power – Kneeling Low in Prayer Standing Tall in God

Praying the Price

PRAYER POWER

Changing the World and You

by

Stuart Robinson

Award Winning & Best Selling Author

CHI
BOOKS

CHI–Books
PO Box 6462
Upper Mt Gravatt, Brisbane
QLD 4122
Australia

www.chibooks.org
publisher@chibooks.org

Prayer Power — Changing the World and You
Copyright © 2023 by Stuart Robinson

Print ISBN: 978-0-6485108-9-5
eBook ISBN: 978-0-6458782-0-2

Under International Copyright Law, all rights reserved. No part of this book may be reproduced, stored in a retrieval system, or transmitted in any form, including by any means electronic, mechanical, photocopying or otherwise in whole or in part without permission in writing from the publisher, except in the case of sermon preparation, reviews or articles and brief quotations embodied in critical articles. The use of occasional page copying for personal or group study is permitted and encouraged. Permission will be granted upon request.

All Scripture quotations, unless otherwise indicated, are taken from the Holy Bible, New International Version®, NIV®. Copyright ©1973, 1978, 1984, 2011 by Biblica, Inc.™ Used by permission of Zondervan. All rights reserved worldwide.

Distributed globally by Ingram Book Group.

CHI-Books is the publishing imprint of CityHarvest International.

Editorial assistance: Anne Hamilton

Cover design: David Stone

Layout: Jonathan Gould

CONTENTS

DEDICATION

This book is dedicated to:

Those faithful intercessors, unseen on earth but well-known in heaven, without whose support little might have been achieved by God through my wife and me over the last six decades of ministry.

The behind-the-scenes team of workers who have taken each of my manuscripts to produce well-presented books.

My friend Liu, the chief proofreader, who with others has worked meticulously correcting my many mistakes, to save me from endless embarrassment.

Foreword

Our earth is just a tiny speck in an overwhelmingly immense universe of an estimated 200 billion trillion stars, including an innumerable array of planets of their own. Our sun, seemingly so powerful, is like one grain of sand from all the beaches of the entire world. We as mere humans may at times rightly wonder if our short lives and busy actions on Earth will make any difference at all in the whole scheme of things. Such musing can lead us to deep fatalism and despair or hopefully drive us into an intimate relationship with the One who created it all. Such closeness with the Lord of the universe, who spoke it all into being, is only possible with the understanding and practice of prayer. If we get to know our Creator and experience how powerful prayer can be, it will give us real significance and dignity as His much beloved children. It will also enable our lives to take on a real sense of meaning and even adventure as we take up the unique missions that He has in store for each one of us. Prayer will not only change us, but it will change our world!

Stuart Robinson's book, *Prayer Power – Changing the World and You,* reflects his more than sixty years of walking with God, learning the lessons of intimacy in prayer as a youth athlete, would-be psychologist, a cross-cultural worker, a pastor of one of Australia's larger churches as well as his worldwide ministry in 70 countries. Robinson has written a magnificent *tour de force* for those wanting to go deeper and farther in prayer. His book is full of uplifting quotes, amazing stories as well as practical suggestions about practicing the kind of intimate, listening, and transformative prayer that connects us to the One on the throne of the universe. He so helpfully demonstrates how our awesome God wants to guide and empower our lives, not only changing us but also the history of our communities, nations, and world.

Normally when writing an endorsement for an author, I will skim through the book and jot down a few sentences of approval to move on to the next thing on my agenda; however, as I began reading Robinson's book with its jaw-dropping stories drawn from his own and others' experience, it was hard for me to put it aside and I found myself having to read and ponder much of the content. I am also now sharing some of the quotes with others to encourage them in their prayer lives. What comes through loud and clear is that our prayers, though we sometimes feel them to be so impotent that they bounce back from the ceiling, are actively being sought out and attentively listened to by our all-knowing and caring God, who welcomes even a whimper arising from our lips or an unspoken anxious thought directed heavenward.

Another thing I appreciate about the book is that it is not just the author's own perspective based on pet Scripture verses or experiences he himself has had. Instead, he includes a vast collection of wise viewpoints and lessons others have learned, coming from both well-known people of prayer as well as some of whom you probably have never heard. The impression one gets in going through it is that it is a virtual panoply of knowledge and experience from the international Body of Christ through history. We all only "see in part", and so it helps to aggregate many partial glimpses and impressions of what communication with the Creator is all about. We can never know it all on this side of eternity, but Robinson has assembled some gleaming guideposts to better point the way.

In his first chapter, *Praying the Price*, he describes some of the great transformations of nations that have occurred as believers have persistently sought the Lord in prayer until sweeping revivals brought moral reformation and restoration to change their hopelessly perverse, decrepit societies. The inflow of God's manifest presence in answer to earnest, believing intercession has transformed some of the most discouraging and dark cultures the world has ever known. How encouraging it is to review such breakthroughs as we consider the desperate situation our current world is in! Robinson counsels, "If things are going to change in the West, it's time for us to accept the challenge of extraordinary prayer. Prayer is not an easy way of getting what we want. It is the only way for our nations and us to become what God wants."

The book goes on to review some of the blocks to effective prayer that lie in ourselves due to sin, relational problems with others, unbelief, lack of forgiveness and other hindrances and how to overcome such impediments. How we need this kind of introspection as we approach our awesome and holy Creator!

Another helpful theme in the book is that real intercession can be costly since it brings us into conflict with the powers that be—those spiritual principalities and powers that, as fallen angelic beings, seek to seduce and dominate humanity in service to the "prince of this world", who is also a "liar and murderer from the beginning" as Jesus called him. Understanding and using the authority that the Lord Jesus delegated to "bind the strongman" and carry out a Spirit-given battle plan for the atmospheric liberation and transformation of cities and other territories is an important emphasis. Robinson also deals with the issue of "spiritual mapping" by which intercessors and ministry workers identify any controlling spirits so they can pray appropriately and authoritatively. Examples and case studies from various cities and nations provide useful guidance from ministry workers who have implemented Jesus' call to use His authority to "tread on serpents and scorpions and to overcome all the power of the enemy" (Luke 10:19).

The author, as a former missionary, is mindful of how essential the linkage of prayer is to the Great Commission and the reaching of the unreached peoples of our world, devoting a chapter to that all-important theme. He tells the story of prayer breakthroughs, as with the Lisu of southwest China and the Magar of Nepal. Adoption of unreached people groups through ongoing prayer by churches and other ministries will make a huge difference for protection, guidance, and favor for missionaries as well as in receptivity to the gospel by the people groups they are trying to reach.

His chapter on revival focuses on breaking free from the liturgical "we have always done it this way" kind of bondage that many churches find themselves in. He concludes that it is by getting back to the early church model of constant, united prayer that unleashed the power of the Holy Spirit in the book of Acts and has done so in all subsequent revival outpourings. He refers to the Brownsville revival in Pensacola, Florida, as a modern-day example and affirms: "From Pentecost in Acts 2 to the present, there is seldom a record of a prayerless revival. Prayer is the key which unlocks the vaults of heaven."

A good summarizing word Robinson leaves us with at the end of the book is: "The God we serve brings life out of death. He is all-powerful, all-knowing, and ever present. He is sovereign over all. He chooses that we should cooperate with Him to fulfill His purposes. For revival our part is to pray. Prayer is the point at which the sovereignty of God meets the responsibility of humankind. We become the conduits of His glory that attracts others to enquire what these things mean."

I have been stirred and inspired by reading it and know you will be as well!

John Robb
Chairman, Transformation Prayer Foundation
Founder, International Prayer Connect and International Prayer Council
Facilitator, World Prayer Assembly (2012)

Introduction

There has never been a significant outpouring of the Holy Spirit on the mission field without a previous outpouring of the human spirit in preparatory prayer.

Oswald Sanders (1902-1992)[1]

In 2018 it was estimated that Africa had become the continent on which most Christians now lived. It had surpassed South America, which had risen to the premier position in the latter half of the twentieth century.

The Western world of Europe, North America, Australia and New Zealand had long since surrendered their claim of preeminence in matters relating to Christianity. In those regions for some decades, Christianity has been on an accelerating decline to where they are becoming "the mission field".

Oswald Sanders, quoted above, did not have these continents in mind when, based upon years of experience as the director of an international missionary agency, he understood the relationship between significant Holy Spirit activity and human prayer.

There are many reasons for the West's spiritual decline, but the more obvious include:

- The rise of secular humanism in its many forms.

---

1   Alan Webb, *Unleashing the Power of Prayer.* East Asia's Millions, Vol.104, No.2. 2.

- The assumption that science will produce solutions to all life's challenges and answer all our questions.
- Materialism, that values people for what they have rather than who they are.
- Affluence, that relegates dependence upon the Almighty to little more than a footnote of history, an outdated concept once held by our less educated forebears.

Furthermore, in the event of sudden need, there is always the largesse of the welfare state, with its safety net cushioning unwelcome blows from cradle to grave. So, who needs God?

Such a potent concoction is toxic to healthy spirituality. The compound of its elements results in asphyxiation of that body that represents the Kingdom of God on earth—the church.

There has never been a generation of God's people like the present church of the West. Its clergy are so highly educated. Its organization is admirably efficient. Its buildings are more comfortable. Its technology for producing and broadcasting its message is unsurpassed. Its position in society in some countries is even protected by law. Yet decade after decade it continues to decline. The very civilization that once derived its foundational values from Christianity, while tolerating its presence, now ignores or rejects its message.

Meanwhile elsewhere in the world, wherever the church is growing exponentially, there are always three prominent characteristics:

1. Persistent prayer.
2. Poverty.
3. Persecution.

Apart from comparatively few isolated examples, all these elements are missing within the Western version of Christianity.

Unless we join religious orders and take vows of poverty, that state is not self-induced. If we do not engage in extreme civil disobedience or break the law of the land, it is unlikely we shall suffer the wrath of our elected governments, which we might interpret as persecution.

To attract the favor of God which rests upon other peoples, that leaves us with the sole possibility of persistent prayer. But observers from poorer countries might be justified in concluding that, in the West, the church places more importance on air conditioning than prayer conditioning. Prayer is a spiritual exercise in which humans don't automatically participate.

In Islam, to miss just one of the five daily obligatory prayer times, Muslims say the punishment is thousands of years in hell. Even with such an ominous threat, many of them still neglect prayer. In the Christian West, our record is little better unless there is some life-threatening crisis which is unsolvable with our own resources.

It has been well said that people who change the course of history are not really presidents, kings or queens. Rather it is those who mobilize the church to pray. In the eighteenth century with Christianity in serious decline in England, John Wesley was used to turn England back toward God. In so doing he saved the nation from the fate of France, that endured a blood drenched Revolution from which, to this day, the church in that country has never recovered.

Based upon his own experience, commenting on Philippians 4:6, in his journal Wesley wrote, "I am persuaded that God does everything by prayer and nothing without it."[2]

Billy Graham knew this. In 1983 at an evangelism conference in Amsterdam hosted by him, he said that there are three basic steps to success in God's eyes:

2 *Praying Things Through Before They Happen.* Australia, Derek Prince Ministries, December 19, 2012.

1. Prayer.
2. Prayer.
3. Prayer.

In the closing decades of the twentieth century, others joined a chorus calling the church to prayer. Ed Silvoso in Argentina, John Dawson from New Zealand, and in America, David Bryant (Concerts of Prayer), Joe Aldrich (Prayer Summits), Dick Eastman (Schools of Prayer), were all among the many who made great contributions to encourage prayer.

Probably a more widespread impact was made by C. Peter Wagner. In 1992, as coordinator of the AD2000 movement's United Prayer Track, he called for a million intercessors to pray for effective evangelism of the 62 countries least reached with the Gospel. More than 20 million intercessors from 105 nations joined in.

The spiritual response was immediate. Reports flooded in testifying to a greater freedom for the Gospel in previously barren harvest fields. Dreams and visions became common. Demonic powers seemed weakened.

In October 1995, a second call to pray was launched and 36.7 million believers joined in. Again, there were frequent reports of miracles and other unusual spiritual manifestations. The church in Africa and Asia grew accordingly.[3]

But in the West…?

In 1998, one of my own books on prayer was published. It was called, *Positioning for Power*. It sold well. I moved on to writing other books while pastoring Crossway, a church in Australia. Repeated calls have been made for an updated edition of *Positioning for Power*. The book that you hold is not an "update". While there are some of the former book's chapter

---

3 *Praying Through the Window III—The Unreached Peoples*. Christian Information Network, Colorado Springs USA, http://www.christian-info.com.

headings and occasionally selections of content, this is basically a new book.

If things are going to change in the West, it's time for us to accept the challenge of extraordinary prayer. Prayer is not an easy way of getting what we want. It is the only way for our nations and us to become what God wants.

Let's get started.

Chapter 1
PRAYING THE PRICE

God is limited by only two things–
unbelief and lack of prayer.

John Wesley (1703-1791)

In 1952, Albert Einstein was asked by a Princeton student what he should research for his doctoral dissertation. Einstein replied, "Find out about prayer."

When English preacher, Sidlow Baxter was 85 years of age he said, "I have pastored only three churches in my more than sixty years of ministry. We had revival in every one. Not one of them came as a result of my preaching. They came as a result of the membership entering a covenant to pray until revival came. And it did come, every time."[4]

Former Chaplain of the United States Senate, Richard Halverson noted that without prayer we are doomed to failure. "You can organize until you are exhausted. You can plan, program and subsidize all your plans. But if you fail to pray, it is a waste of time. Prayer is not optional. It is mandatory. Not to pray is to disobey God."[5]

In what is today known as South Korea, in the twentieth century the church grew from 1.8% to 40.8% of the population. In China a similar phenomenon is occurring. In mainland China's 1953 census, Christians were numbered at 660,000.

---

4   Bob Willhite, *Why Pray?* Altamonte Springs, Florida, Creation House, 1988, 111.
5   David Bryant, *Concerts of Prayer.* Ventura, California, Regal Books, 1984, 39.

No one can be sure of the current number of believers in China today. But early in 2008 speaking in Beijing University, a government official of the Department of Religious Affairs, announced that while the Government couldn't be certain, the number of Christians could be as many as 130 million. In both countries Christian leaders identify one element being more important than any other—persistent, persevering prayer.

Pastor David Yonggi Cho whose church in Seoul grew to approximately a million members before he retired, said that any church could see this sort of phenomenal growth if they were prepared to "pray and obey". In South Korea it is normal for believers to go to bed early to rise by 4:00am, to be in church by 5:00am, to participate in corporate prayer. It is normal to pray throughout Friday nights to 6:00am Saturday. It is normal to use the first three days of their nine days annual holiday leave at prayer retreats.

In these countries prayer is a way of life, not just a crash response to an emergency.

Supernatural Growth

Only God causes things to grow (1 Corinthians 3:7). A church is no exception to this principle. It also is a living organism. Jesus Christ is its head (Colossians 1:18). From Him life flows (John 14:6). Our part is to cooperate with Him (1 Corinthians 3:6). Unless the Lord builds the house, we labor in vain (Psalm 127:1). To transfer a single soul from the kingdom of darkness to the kingdom of light from beginning to end is a supernatural process (Colossians 1:13).

It is the Father who draws (John 6:44).

It is the Holy Spirit who convicts (John 16:8-11).

The Holy Spirit causes confession to be made (1 Corinthians 12:3).

The Holy Spirit completes conversion (Titus 3:5).

The Holy Spirit strengthens and empowers (Ephesians 3:16).

The Holy Spirit guides into truth (John 16:13).

The Holy Spirit gives spiritual gifts that promote unity (1Corinthians 12:15).

This builds up the Church thus avoiding disunity and strife (1Corinthians 14:12).

These fundamentals are believed by all Christians. However, the degree to which we are willing to act upon these beliefs will be reflected by the priority we give to participating in personal and the corporate prayer of the church. It is only when we realize that nothing of significance happens apart from prayer, that prayer will become more than an occasional meeting for the faithful few of the local congregation. It will become a response of obedience to a Biblical imperative.

Biblical Imperative

In the Old Testament, excluding the Psalms, there are 77 explicit references to prayer. But in the far briefer span of history covered in the New Testament, the spiritual temperature heats up. There are 94 references directly relating to Jesus and prayer. The Apostles followed the example of Jesus.

Paul commands, "Pray continually, for this is God's will for you" (1 Thessalonians 5:17–18).

Peter urges believers to be "clear minded and self-controlled" so that they can pray (1 Peter 4:7).

James declares that prayer is "powerful and effective" (James 5:17–18).

John assures us that "God hears and answers" (1 John 5:15).

The Acts of the Apostles record 36 instances of the early church growing. In 21 of those instances, it is in the context of prayer.

Many long to see growth in their church like Pentecost and soon after. The key to that possibility is in Acts 1:14. "They (were) all joined together constantly in prayer." They were singularly united in purpose and intent. They were persistent in their practice of persevering prayer.

Acts 2:42 sums it up. "They devoted themselves...to prayer."

Years later Paul urges the newest generation of believers to do likewise. "Devote yourselves to prayer" (Colossians 4:2).

Every significant era of accelerated growth of the church in history has been preceded by the implementation of the same prayer principle.

In History

In 1722, persecuted Moravian Brethren found refuge in **Germany** under the protection of the Lutheran Christian Count Nicolas von Zinzendorf. They settled at Hutberg (Watch Hill) and renamed it Herrnhut (The Lord's Watch—Isaiah 62:1, 6-7). In August 1727 the power of the Holy Spirit fell upon those gathered in a local parish hall. As a result of this a continuous prayer movement was commenced. It was known as "Hourly Intercession". It was uninterruptedly sustained for 100 years. During that century of continuous prayer, the Moravians commissioned over 100 missionaries who were sent out to more than 50 nations.

It was similar for other founders of international missionary movements. William Carey, Adoniram Judson, David Livingstone, Hudson Taylor and others all received their callings within the contexts of sustained prayer encounters.

During 1895-1925, John R. Mott led a movement known as the Student Christian Movement. From this, 20,000 career missionaries were commissioned. Mott attributed this extraordinary outcome to united intercessory prayer. He testified that these workers were recruited and (financially) sustained–through prayer.

> **The devil fears nothing from prayerless study, work and Christian activity.**

Luther, Calvin, Knox, Latimer, Wesley, Finney, Moody, Cho, all "greats of God", based the effectiveness of their ministries upon persevering prayer.

If I fail to spend two hours in prayer each morning, the devil gets the victory through the day. I have so much to do I cannot get on without spending three hours daily in prayer.

Martin Luther

I have so much to do that I must spend several hours in prayer before I am able to do it all.

John Wesley

Wesley would not ordain candidates for what became the Methodist ministry, unless they first covenanted to fast and pray till 4:00pm every Wednesday and Friday. No denomination in the West today would include this among their qualifications to be ordained for ministry. Could that explain the difference in effectiveness between those of Wesley's generation and ours today?

Samuel Chadwick was of the view that the devil fears nothing from prayerless study, work and Christian activity. Satan laughs at our toil. He mocks our wisdom, but trembles when we pray.

Worse Than Today

Toward the end of the 18th century the spiritual condition in **Europe** was grim. France was soaked in blood as the guillotine loped heads off any who were declared enemies of the revolutionary republic. Voltaire was preaching that the church was only a system for oppressing the human spirit. In accordance with the tenets of the new morality, the Church was held in universal contempt. In **England**, if people dared to speak of Jesus in the public domain, they were pelted with stones, pieces of coal or rotten fruit. But unknown to the masses, long before the nadir of public opprobrium was reached, God was quietly preparing his counterattack.

In 1747, John Erskine wrote a pamphlet entitled, "*A Humble Attempt to Promote Explicit Agreement and Visible Union of God's People in Extraordinary Prayer.*"[6] For the next 40 years through voluminous correspondence, Erskine orchestrated a concert of prayer for God's intervention to rescue the nation from its derelict spiritual state.

When God intends great mercy for His people, He first sets them praying.

On Christmas Eve 1781, at 3:00pm people met in St Just Church in Cornwall to sing and pray. The heavens seemed to open as the Holy Spirit invaded their orderly Church of England service. The predictable liturgical formula was abandoned as worshipers prayed through the night until

---

6   Jonathan Yeager, *The Letters of Jonathan Erskine to the Rylands*. Eusebia, Spring, 2008, 183.

9:00am Christmas Day. Having taken time out for the traditional Christmas lunch, they regathered on Christmas evening. By March 1782 they were praying daily till midnight. It was not preaching which inspired people to continue. It was lay people spontaneously praying as the Holy Spirit responded to their entreaties.

In 1784, when 83-year-old John Wesley rode through the area he wrote, "This country is all on fire and the flame is spreading from village to village." Like wildfire, it spread uncontrollably.

Matthew Henry wrote, "When God intends great mercy for His people, He first sets them praying."

Across the country prayer meetings multiplied and networked to pray for national revival. Baptist churches in Northampton, Leicester and the Midlands set aside regular nights focused on prayer for revival. Methodists and Anglicans joined in.

Within the context of such widespread intense prayer two other phenomena commonly occur—passion for evangelism and supernatural interventions. Non-believers were committing to Jesus, not through church services to which they had been invited, but in prayer meetings to which they had been attracted. For some that occurred through dreams and visions. For others when they arrived to scoff, they were thrown to the ground by the undeniable power of the Holy Spirit.

Some meetings were at 5:00am. Others were at midnight. Some were a cacophony of noise and confusion. Others were characterized by solemn still silence. But always there was the operation of the Holy Spirit bringing people to Jesus. Whole denominations doubled, tripled and then quadrupled within a few years.

National Transformation

Changed lives inevitably caused change in society. William Wilberforce, William Pitt, Edmund Bourke and Charles Fox, all worked ceaselessly to abolish the slave trade till it happened in 1807. William Buxton pressed on till all slaves in the British Empire were emancipated in 1834.

John Howard and Elizabeth Fry toiled to have the prison system overhauled and reformed. Florence Nightingale likewise worked to change hospital care radically. She established the principles and practice of modern nursing.

The Seventh Earl of Shaftesbury, Ashley Cooper, improved the lives of the poor by having labor laws reformed. Before this, workers ground out 16-hour days, 7 days a week. He also worked to stamp out the exploitation of women and children deep underground in coalmines. Above ground he was able to stop the use of boys as chimney sweeps, which often resulted in their death from breathing in chimney dust.

Having won a rest day for laborers, Cooper established for their further enjoyment public parks, gardens, gymnasia, public libraries, night schools and choral societies.

The Christian Socialist Movement that morphed into the British Trade Union movement was formed. Even the welfare of animals was positively affected by the revival through the founding of the Royal Society for the Prevention of Cruelty of Animals (RSPCA).

William Carey was a member of a minister's revival prayer group meeting in Northampton in 1784–1786. Deeply touched, he shared his vision for the lost in other countries. He fulfilled his own vision by becoming the founder of the Baptist Missionary Society. In 1795, the London Missionary Society was birthed as was the Scottish Missionary Society. The Anglicans followed suit with the Church Missionary Society.

All of this and much more occurred in part because one man, John Erskine, persisted, encouraged and nourished prayer cells across the nation, beseeching God for revival—for 40 years!

North America

The spiritual climate in North America was similar to what had been the case in the United Kingdom. The trauma of the American Revolution seemed to have left people to slump into a moral swamp. Of a population of five million, 300,000 were confirmed drunkards. Profanities peppered the discourse of the common man. Bank robberies were a daily occurrence.

At Harvard, founded to educate men for ministry, not one believer could be identified on the whole campus. At the more evangelical campus of Princeton, two believers were found. Students conducted anti-Christian plays. They stole a Bible from a Presbyterian church and used it as fuel for a public bonfire. The Chief Justice of Virginia wrote, "The Church is too far gone ever to be redeemed." Over in continental Europe French philosopher, Voltaire gloated, "Christianity will be forgotten in 30 years."

In 1794, New England pastor, Isaac Backus, issued a plea for all denominations in the country to unite in prayer for Revival. The era's most influential preacher, Jonathan Edwards, wrote a book with a title as lofty as the book's objective, *"A humble attempt to promote explicit agreement and visible union of all God's people in extraordinary prayer for the revival of religion and the advancement of Christ's Kingdom."*

Across America prayer meetings for revival were held in churches on the first Monday of every month. The answer was not long in coming. Revival fires came first to Connecticut and Massachusetts. By 1800, there was revival in Kentucky and from there across the frontier. As in the UK, missionary movements were birthed along with the abolition of slavery, education of children and various other social benefits.

However, as was recorded in the various accounts in the Bible, spiritual high points inevitably degenerate with the natural onset of spiritual entropy. Thus, by the middle of the nineteenth century, again the situation was grim. An economic depression caused the all-important railroad construction projects to cease. Factory output declined. Unemployment soared. Banks were failing. Church life was declining and was as depressed as the national economy.

Then God lit a spark in distant Hamilton, Ontario, in Canada. News of it reached New York. Could there yet be hope for New York?

In that city, the North Reformed Dutch Church, hardly famous for passion for exuberant outreach, appointed a layman to develop a program of evangelism. Jeremiah Lamphier was a businessman who had decided to reject the success syndrome that drives businesspeople the world over. Having stepped off the treadmill of commercial success, he sought God in how to carry out this new appointment. His prayer was simple, "Lord, what wilt Thou have me to do?"[7]

When no other solution presented itself Lamphier did the obvious. He started with prayer. He put up posters announcing a noontime prayer meeting in the Old Dutch Church in Fulton Street. The first one was scheduled for September 23, 1857.

At the appointed time Lamphier sat alone. Eventually one man showed up followed by five others. Next week there were 20. The third week there were 40. The meetings changed from weekly to daily. Within a few months other meetings multiplied throughout the city. Within six months offices and stores had to close at midday as 10,000 staff went off to pray.

---

7   John Woodbridge, ed., *More Than Conquerors*. Chicago, Illinois, Moody Press, 1992, 337.

Newspapers spread the story of the prayer revival in New York. Telegraph companies reserved certain hours for businessmen to wire news of the emerging event to acquaintances in other cities. By the spring of 1858, 2,000 men were meeting daily to pray in Chicago's Metropolitan Theatre. Philadelphia, Baltimore, Washington, Cincinnati, New Orleans and Mobile were quick to follow.

In New York as people prayed, 10,000 people were being converted every week. It was not so much in response to preachers' sermons. It was the Holy Spirit manifesting the power of God through the prayers of His people. In a nation of 30 million people, one million were converted in just 12 months.

The movement swept out to fan cooling embers in England, Scotland, Wales and Ulster.

Over in **Northern Ireland**, James McQuilkin gathered three young men on March 14, 1859. In the Kells school they prayed that the revival in America would come to their land. Within months other prayer meetings were launched to pray for revival. On September 21, 20,000 people gathered for the same purpose.

It was estimated that 100,000 conversions directly resulted from the prayer movement in Ireland.

By 1900, realizing the need once more, people started to pray for another visitation of the Lord through His church. In the UK, Australia, India and Korea, they humbled themselves, confessed their sins and united in prayer seeking God's favor.

By 1905, in Portland, Oregon, 240 department stores closed from 11:00am to 2:00pm daily to enable their staff to attend prayer meetings. God honored their persistence.

In Atlantic City in a population of 50,000, only 50 people remained unconverted. In the University of California Los

Angeles campus (UCLA), 25% of students were enrolled in Bible study groups.

As a result of a prayer movement in **Wales**, revival exploded in 1904. In five months, 100,000 people were converted. Again, there were no preachers. It was characterized by multiple prayer meetings. As before there were profound social impacts. The number of babies conceived outside of marriage declined by 44% in one year. Drunkenness was reduced by 50%. Crime almost ceased. Police were underemployed. Human behavior was so altered that even mules used in the coalmines became confused, because the miners were no longer abusing and mistreating them.

In 1949, the population on the island of Lewis in the **Scottish Hebrides** was 37,000. The church was dying. Two women aged 82 and 84 concerned about state of their parish of Bravas, commenced to pray from 10:00pm to 4:00am twice a week. They eventually challenged the leadership of their church to do likewise. They agreed.

Six weeks later the power of God fell on the parish. Work stopped in fields, farms and weaving looms. Dance halls emptied. On the roadside young men knelt and begged God for mercy. People crowded into formerly neglected churches. One participant noted that 75% of those who became believers made their commitment before they came near any church.

In the same year of the Lord's visitation to the Scottish Hebrides in answer to their prayer, it seemed that in far off **Argentina** God had forgotten that nation. Missionary Edward Miller was so depressed at the lack of responsiveness to their mission's best efforts, he considered resigning and returning to America. Instead, encouraged by Scriptural promises, he determined to spend eight hours a day in prayer and Bible study.

Days became months. Nothing happened. Miller prayed on. Then he was led to announce a prayer meeting each Monday night from 8:00pm to midnight. Only three others turned up. In answer to their intercession, on the fourth night the Spirit descended upon the small group who were praying in the town of Mendoza. Hearing something was happening, new people started to arrive. They were touched powerfully by the Holy Spirit. Within weeks membership of the church quadrupled. Spirit-empowered teams fanned out. A movement was underway.

Then in 1951, the Spirit touched a young, barely educated, indigenous tearaway named Alexander. Although he had been well-known for his drunkenness, he had been totally transformed because of his divine encounter. He enrolled in a Bible school in City Bell and continued praying fervently for his nation. On June 4 ,1951, there was the first of many angelic appearances during which it was revealed the Lord would visit many cities in response to their prayers at the Bible College.

In the far-off **United States**, another angel appeared to an unknown, untrained man. Tommy Hicks had been praying and fasting for revival for months. The angel ordered him to go to Argentina. Through a series of miraculous events, this hitherto unknown man ended up preaching nightly to 200,000 people every night in the famous Huracan Stadium in Buenos Aires.

So great was the power of God in those meetings, that people from all over South America flocked to gain entrance. After a few months, an exhausted Hicks knew his mission was over. He returned to anonymity in the United States. But Argentina had been transformed. Massive mega-churches led often by pastors with little formal education sprang into existence. They led the continuation of the revival through prayer and fasting.[8]

---

8   R. Edward Miller, *Thy God Reigneth—The Story of Revival in Argentina*. Burbank, California, World Missionary Assistance Plan, 1964.

In January 1959, communist insurgents led by Fidel Castro, drove dictator Fulgencio Batista from **Cuba**. Instead of delivering on his promise of religious freedom, within two years Christian activities were suppressed. Churches were destroyed. Pastors were imprisoned. But believers knew that by kneeling low in prayer, they would stand tall in God.

In 1987, Pastor Juan received a vision of Jesus visiting Cuba. He commenced a 24/7 prayer meeting in his church. Two days per week were also set aside for fasting. By the end of 1988, 100,000 people were involved in the prayer movement.

Then, in the small town of Mardruga, in one of those prayer meetings a lame man was healed. The news spread. People started to queue to gain entrance to the prayer meetings. In a single weekend 8,000 came. By 1991, miracles were being reported throughout Cuba from all denominations. The church grew to embrace more than a million believers.[9]

> **Believers knew that by kneeling low in prayer, they would stand tall in God.**

During the three decades of Fidel Castro's reign, Southern Baptist Churches grew from 210 to 238—an increase of only 28 in 30 years. By 2010, their number of churches exceeded 6,200! Construction of worship centers could not keep pace in accommodating new believers.[10] In the period 1995-2015, more than 16,000 additional evangelical churches commenced operating.[11]

---

9   Open Doors, *Cuba for Christ*. Tonbridge, UK, Sovereign World, 1999, 12.

10   OpenHeaven.com—*Cuba is seeing one of the fastest growth rates in the world*. http://www.openheaven.com/forums/printer_friendly_posts. asp?FID=3&TID=34754, November 28, 2010.

11   Dan Wooding, *How Suffering Made Cuba's Churches Grow*. http://assistnews.net/ index.php/component/k2/item/981-how-suffering-made-cubas-churches-grow. September 12, 2015. (https://www.youtube.com/watch?v=r9-4bqZhxts)

Asked to explain what was happening, local people replied, "We have suffered for the Gospel and we have prayed for many, many years."[12]

Nepal was exclusively a Hindu kingdom. But in 1951 the Rana regime was overthrown. King Tribhuvan opened the borders. But laws banning proselytization remained in place. The first Christian mission to be granted permission to operate was the United Mission to Nepal (UMN). Laws banning evangelism were reaffirmed as recently as 2017.

> Prayer walking is a powerful component of spiritual warfare.

In 1966, there were an estimated 100 national baptized believers. By 1980, that number had increased to 7,000. By 1990, it was 50,000.[13] By 2015, there were an estimated 1 million believers.[14]

One survey concluded that the Nepali church had become the fastest growing church in the world.[15]

All of this was happening despite national hostility and persecution of believers and pastors. Research conducted by Christian and non-Christian scholars, concluded that the main reason for such a phenomenon was supernatural healings and prayer.[16]

---

12   Greg O'Connor, *Miracles in Cuba*. New Day, May 1990, 7–9.
13   Norma Kehrberg, *The Cross in the Land of the Khukuri*. Kathmandu, Elka Books, 2000, 124.
14   Ian Gibson, David Gellner, Ramon Saro, *Suffering and Christianity: conversion and ethical change among the Newars of Bhaktapur*. https://ora.ox.ac.uk/objects/ uuid:3eea0dc1-3f8e-4564-887f-f7aae26de57f, 2015, viewed December 10, 2021.
15   Gordon-Conwell Theological Seminary, *Christianity in its Global Context, 1970-2020: Society, Religion and Mission*. South Hamilton, MA, Center for the Study of Global Christianity, 38, viewed January 27, 2019.
16   Ian Gibson, *Suffering and Hope: Christianity and Ethics Among the Newars of Bhaktapur*. Kathmandu, Ekta, 2017, Chapter 7.

The prayer factor was not a recently introduced element. In October 1993, 4,700 intercessors were identified as praying for Nepal. At the same time, 12 external prayer teams were entering the country to increase prayer pressure over the country.[17]

In **Brazil** in 1991, Protestants comprised only nine percent of the population. But by the time of the 2010 census their number had exploded to represent more than 22.2% of the population. From the 2020 census, it was estimated that number had increased to 31%—i.e., 65 million people making it one of the world's largest concentrations of believers.[18]

By way of explanation of this amazing transformation, national leaders said it owed "much to the powerful prayer support undergirding everything… Anna Maria de Castro (led) networks of a prayer movement of more than 10,000 intercessors."[19]

One observer identified the essential role of prayer walking. This involved intercessors saturating a targeted area by walking through it, praying as they go, before any outreach activity was commenced. "Communities bound by the enemy must be freed up and released from the hold of the strong man! When this happens the first phase of a church planting strategy has been successfully undertaken."[20]

Prayer walking has become an essential element of strategic outreach in all non-Western continents.

"God's Kingdom cannot advance unless we take the territory from the enemy and this can only happen through the strategic use of prayer," said one leader in **India**.

---

17   Luis Bush, *Reaching every people group in Nepal for Christ.* MARC Newsletter No. 96-1, March 1996, 6.

18   *50% dos brasileiros são católicos, 31% evangélicos e 10% nãotêm religîao, diz Datafolha,* (viewed December 1, 2021).

19   Berna Salcedo *Explosive growth in Brazil will make 250,000 churches a reality.* Dawn Ministries, Issue 2 Vo.1, November 2005, 5.

20   Ted Olsen, *The story of DAWN is the saga of the exploding Church.* Dawn Around the World, Issue 2, Vol.1, November 2005, 4.

One team reported that a Hindu temple god made of granite, cracked in two as they walked and prayed in a specific area. A local leader described the process thus:

When we go out to prayer walk, we are actually binding the powers of darkness operating in that realm... which is multi-faceted and deeply entrenched... We bind the powers of darkness and loose the grace of God... Prayer walking is a powerful component of spiritual warfare.[21]

This leader spoke from experience. Previously he had led his team using traditional outreach methods introduced by Western missionaries. For some months he and his team visited 750,000 homes in their region. To the inhabitants of each home they preached, testified and left some Christian literature. This resulted in only two people accepting their message. Clearly this methodology, although practiced and led by Westerners for many years, was never going to win the nation.

The leader withdrew to seek the mind of God through prayer and fasting. After some months he emerged to implement a new plan that changed everything—especially the results.

In 2015, they baptized 72,167 new believers. In 2017, that number increased to 76,274. They were planting 16 new churches a day. Then an increasingly hostile environment emerged. But the foundation of this emerging movement did not change. The leader summed up the "secret" of what was happening in three words. "Intimacy with Jesus." "Without Me you can do nothing." (John 15:5)

The power of constant prayer undergirds everything.

On a national scale the same principle saw the Christian population in today's **South Korea** grow from virtually zero to approximately 40% in the twentieth century.

---

21   *When prayer walking is an essential component of church planting.* Dawn Around the World, Dawn Ministries, Issue 2 Vol.1, November 2005, 3.

Similarly in **China**, according to Professor Feng Gang Yang of Purdue University, the number of Christians in China could be 247 million by 2030, despite one of the more oppressive Communist regimes implacably opposing Christianity. The world has never seen a church like that which the Lord is building in China. And in the West, we have not given ourselves over to prayer as is practiced in China.

> The great need of our day is prayer, more prayer, better prayer.

Years ago R.A.Torrey said, "We live in a day characterized by the multiplication of man's machinery and the diminution of God's power. The great cry of our day is work, work, work! Organize, organize, organize! Give us some new methods! Devise some new machinery! But the great need of our day is prayer, more prayer, better prayer."[22]

He said that a century ago. Since then, we have invented technologies of which Torrey could never have dreamed. In every one of the nations that are wealthiest with the most advanced economies, educational levels and technologies, the church is slowly dying, lurching toward an abyss of its own extinction. From atop our own glass and steel towers of Babel, we are discovering that God seems less accessible in our man-made world. Surrounded by monuments of our own ingenuity, we grow deaf to the echoes of eternity.

With the Webb Telescope we can see billions of miles into space. But we cannot see the hand of God in our own lives. We can communicate with robots on Mars but seem to have forgotten how to communicate with the Lord of the earth. If that is so, our only hope is to humble ourselves as did the first disciples, to kneel and beg, "Lord, teach us to pray." (Luke 11:1)

22   *Prayer: No. 1 issue in churches, survey of leaders shows.* www.hapnews.org. April 12, 2005.

Chapter 2
WHY PRAY?

*It is not that prayer changes God or awakens
in Him purposes of love and compassion that
He has not already felt. No, it changes us,
and therein lies its glory and its purpose.*

Hannah Hurnard (1905-1990)

In a small conservative Midwestern American town, a tavern owner commenced building a new bar to expand his business. A local church, opposed to additional alcohol outlets, campaigned against the construction through petitions to the relevant civic authorities and prayers to God.

The work continued unabated until one week before opening day. It was then that lightning struck the bar, which started a fire that burnt the building to the ground.

The church folk were somewhat smug about this outcome, till the tavern owner commenced legal proceedings against the church. His case was that the church was ultimately responsible, directly or indirectly, for the demolition of his building and the destruction of his business. In the church's defense, they pleaded denial of all responsibility for what had happened. They insisted the event had no connection with them whatsoever.

At the opening of the case in the local court, the judge appointed to hear and decide the matter, having read the written submissions advised the contesting parties, "I don't know how I'm going to decide this matter. It appears we have a bar owner who believes in the power of prayer and a church that doesn't!"

Given the demise of many churches, the judge's humorous observation may have been more accurate than he imagined. When it comes to prayer, our lack of its serious practice, says more about our ignorance than our words affirming its importance.

An African tribal warrior was walking through a forest when he saw a peculiar shaped stick leaning against a tree trunk. He picked it up and took it home with him. Not knowing what to do with it, he leaned it against the wall of his house, hoping that someday somebody might be able to explain how it was to be used.

Months later a friend arrived on a visit. Noticing the "stick" leaning against the wall, he asked where it had been found. Later, taking the "stick" with them, the visitor demonstrated its usefulness in hunting wild animals. Raising the "stick" to his shoulder, the visitor pointed it at a distant animal and moved his forefinger. There was a deafening noise and in the distance the animal fell dead. The warrior was astonished as his visitor explained to him that his "stick" was a high-powered rifle. He exclaimed, "To think I had this power in my hands all this time and I did not use it."[23]

The same could be said of many Christians with respect to personal prayer. We tend to be neglectful of its usage unless there is an emergency beyond our ability to control.

A sign in a Nebraska (USA) high school building read: "In the event of an earthquake or tornado the Supreme Court ruling against prayer in school will be temporarily suspended."

We sometimes regard prayer as little more than the spiritual version of an intercom system at fast food drive-ins. Into these

---

23   Egerton C. Long, *Prayer what's it all about.* Glenhaven, NSW, Australia, 1984, 3.

we speak our request, drive around the corner to the delivery window and within minutes, we take off enjoying our salty trans-fat food on our way to obesity and our first heart attack.

Others think of God as the great vending machine operator in the sky. Put in a coin-sized prayer and hey presto—out pops the answer as a reward for being a good person. Unfortunately, the reality is somewhat more complex.

Attempts to define prayer often result in providing a list of exceptions longer than the definition. George Peters has made one of the more comprehensive attempts. He says, "Prayer (is) more than a recital of formulas or the practice of rituals. It (is) the expression of a kinship relationship, dependence, anticipation, confidence and assurance, not only in the existence of God, but in His ability to change the course of history and to direct the ways of people."[24]

He might have added that it also changes us—when we pray.

So why should we pray?

1. The Example of Jesus

Any sincere Christian longs to be more like Jesus. And why not? It is a goal referred to in Scripture (Romans 6:4; Philippians 3:21; 1 John 3:2). In His practice of prayer what do we find? He prayed:

- When the Holy Spirit anointed Him for service (Luke 3:21-22).
- After an exhausting day of ministry (Mark 1:34-35).
- During times of pressure and stress (Luke 5:15-16).
- Prior to important decisions (Luke 6:12-13).
- Offering His life for others (Matthew 14:22-23; Mark 6:45-46).

---

24   George W. Peters, *A Theology of Church Growth*. Grand Rapids, MI, Zondervan, 1981, 156.

- Before asking His disciples about His identity (Luke 9:18-20).
- Preceding the appearance of Moses and Elijah (Luke 9:29-30).
- In thanking the Father for revelation (Luke 10:21-22).
- When the disciples recognized their need to pray (Luke 11:1).
- Thanksgiving for answered prayer (John 11:41-42).
- Surrendering His will (Luke 22:41-42).
- Interceding for us (John 17:1-26).
- For strength during crises (Matthew 26:39-44; Mark 14:32-39; Luke 21:36).
- On the cross (Luke 23:46).

Not only did Jesus provide a compelling example, but he also commanded his disciples to pray. "Ask...Seek...Knock" (Matthew 7:7-8).

The early church followed our Lord's example and command. For them prayer:

- Provided answers for sensitive decisions (Acts 1:14, 24).
- Gave the apostles boldness in witnessing (Acts 3:1; 4:23-24).
- Released strength to suffer and die for their faith (Acts 7:50-60).
- Enabled believers to be filled with the Holy Spirit (Acts 8:14-15).
- Brought the dead back to life and resulted in other miracles (Acts 9:36-41).
- Defeated Satan's evil intentions (Acts 12:1-17).
- Identified the first cross-cultural workers (Acts 13:1-4).
- Caused prison doors to be opened (Acts 16:25-34).

The certainty and centrality of prayer led to it becoming a command, a matter of obedience for all the New Testament churches (1 Thessalonians 5:17; Colossians 4:2-4). To pray was also a strong admonition (James 5:13-18) that Jesus had previously encouraged (Luke 18:1).

The example and commands of our Lord, the Apostles and the early church should be sufficient for us to do likewise. But often we don't. Why?

That question was put in a lecture at Dallas Theological Seminary being delivered by its first President, Lewis Sperry Chafer. His reply—"Prayer is hard work, and we are inherently lazy." That served as a wake-up call to his class.

> **Prayer is hard work, and we are inherently lazy.**

If prayer is not an easy way of getting what we want, by having God serve our needs and wishes, our egocentricity asks, "Well, what's in it for me?" Why engage, let alone persist? Apart from examples of our forebears, why else should we even begin?

The answer is to be found not from navel-gazing or contemplating unfulfilled desires, fenced in by our exceedingly limited miniaturized world of existence. It's better to view matters from the perspective of the One to whom we pray. He declares there is none like Him (Isaiah 46:9). His greatness no one can fathom (Psalm 145:3). But regardless of our limitations of language, thought and intelligence, we need to start by trying to understand just who it is to whom we pray.

That which distinguishes the God of the Bible from every other claimant to divinity is summed up in three words—"God is love" (1 John 4:8, 16). No other god claims or exhibits this unique characteristic. Love does not exist in total isolation. It requires another outside of itself, who in turn is free to respond to that love. An inanimate object can't respond. Nor can one person be compelled to love another. Otherwise, they would be reduced to automaton status. The most life-like avatar produced by our most advanced use of artificial intelligence, even with the help of quantum computing, is never going to qualify.

For love to exist there needs to be at least two independent beings in voluntary association. From our limited knowledge, that condition has always been in existence with the God of the Bible.

The Bible declares, "God is one" (Deuteronomy 6:4; Mark 12:29). But that "one" can be simple or complex. "One" as used in mathematics is "simple". "One" used to describe a single person or a three-dimension room is a "complex" usage of the same term. In the Bible the Hebrew word "yachid" denotes a mathematical unit—simple unity. The Bible also uses "echad" as "one" to describe complex unity. In Deuteronomy 6:4, to describe God as one "echad" is used.

From beginning to end, the Bible asserts complexity within the unity of the Godhead. In the first verse in Genesis, it declares Elohim as creator. Elohim is a plural word. As the revelation proceeds, we discover that God exists as Father, Son and Holy Spirit. This is consistently reaffirmed right through to the last book in the Bible (Revelation 14:12-13).

It is especially emphasized at the beginning of Jesus' ministry with the involvement of all three entities (Matthew 3:16-17). Lest we forget, Jesus stressed it in commissioning His disciples (Matthew 28:19-20). Love has always been the bonding of the Trinity (John 17:24). In relating to humans each being has a different function. God the Father is for us (Matthew 3:17; Romans 5:8), sending the Son. The Son is God with us, becoming human (John 1:14). The Holy Spirit is God within us, transforming us from within (2 Corinthians 3:18).[25]

---

25   Bernie Power, *Jesus and Muhammad*. Moreland, Australia, Acorn Press, 2016, 29.

In that God is love, understandably the divine priority is relationships. For this reason, we were created and extraordinarily given a capacity to love and the freedom of will to accept or reject God's overtures.

According to the Biblical record (Genesis 2), our forebears were offered the privilege of enjoying a relationship with our Creator based upon a foundation of love. Unfortunately, they were seduced into accepting Satan's counteroffer—power based upon knowledge (Genesis 3:1-5). This delusionary utopian option has mostly mesmerized us ever since, to our own sorrow.

Even so, our relational God still desires to have fellowship with us. That is His eternal desire. For this reason, He sent Jesus on a rescue mission (John 4:34). Through what He did, it has become possible for that fellowship, that was ruptured in Eden, to be restored (John 3:16; Romans 5:8).

2. Fellowship With God

We may say we love another. But if time is not spent in the presence of the other, inevitably the relationship shrivels, dries and dies. It is a truism that absence makes the heart grow fonder—of somebody else.

Through prayer we nourish our relationship with our creator. The essential element in that process is in that which we all have—time. To the degree to which we intentionally set aside time consciously to wait upon God, we demonstrate our obedience to and love for Him. We also predetermine our usefulness for His achieving His goals for us and through us. Whenever we open ourselves to God through prayer, not only is He able to achieve His will through us, but we also are being transformed. The process is like what happens when a luminous watch face is exposed to bright light. It shines in the dark. As the Apostle Paul wrote, "... We... are being transformed into His likeness with ever increasing glory" (2 Corinthians 3:18).

> Our prayer releases
>
> God's power to effect
>
> what He decrees.

That alone should inspire some desire within us—to pray. Out of the development of our relationship with God, He increasingly trusts and uses us to achieve His purposes in the world. When we work, we work. When we pray, God works.

It is a humbling thought to appreciate that Almighty God would choose to work through us to achieve His purposes.

3. He Works Through Us

God works in response to our prayers. This is one of those awesome and mysterious truths found in the Bible.

Some might well ask: in that God is sovereign, doesn't He do whatever He wants to do? Good question. He makes decisions. But it is through our prayers that those decisions are frequently implemented.

In, say, a municipality, decision-making belongs to an authority usually known as the City Council. The Council may decide to widen a road. Therefore, certain houses need to be repossessed and then demolished. When all is ready, the workmen are sent in with the authority of the Council to do the job of implementing the decision and will of the Council.

Similarly, the Lord of heaven and earth has decreed the demolition of Satan's strongholds. As we pray, armed with His authority, the job is done through us (2 Corinthians 10:4; Ephesians 2:10). Our prayer releases God's power to effect what He decrees.

The purpose of our prayer is not to get God to serve us, but for us to join with Him to put into effect His will on earth.

We become His hands and feet, in response to our own prayer (1 Corinthians 3:9; 2 Corinthians 5:20-6:2).

Also, we know that it's God's desire that all peoples of the earth hear the truth about Him and especially what has been achieved through Jesus' death and resurrection. To get that good news out a missionary mouthpiece is needed. "Missionary" literally means "one who is sent" as does "Apostle". Missionary is derived from Latin and Apostle is from the Greek language. The process of what happens is laid out logically in Romans 10:13-15.

> ".... Everyone who calls upon the name of the Lord will be saved.
>
> How then can they call on the one they have not believed in? And how can they believe in the one of whom they have not heard? And how can they hear without someone preaching to them? And how can they preach unless they are sent?"

Certainly, the harvest will be plentiful. But workers will remain too few unless we first pray for them to be sent out (Matthew 9:37-38).

An oft-quoted verse in the Old Testament nicely illustrates the same principle. "If My people, who are called by My name, will humble themselves and pray and seek My face and turn from their wicked ways, then will I hear from heaven and will forgive their sin and will heal their land" (2 Chronicles 7:14).

To express it even more simply, as we pray with the right attitude, God works, doing what only He can do.

Exodus 17:8-13 recounts the story of how the inexperienced Joshua won his battle over the Amalekites. Victory was achieved only as Moses prayed on a nearby hill.

Jesus promised that God will act in response to our prayers (Matthew 18:18). Verified from a lifetime of ministry, the Apostle James reconfirmed the truth of what Jesus had said. James wrote, "The prayer of a righteous man (really) is powerful and effective" (James 5:16).

With the withdrawal of foreign troops from Afghanistan in 2021, swiftly the Taliban were able to retake the capital city of Kabul. Having experienced their type of Islamist government during 1996-2001, fear spread throughout the country. Believers especially had good cause to fear. The Taliban had already declared their intention of implementing Sharia Law. It mandates death for apostasy for adult sane males and indefinite imprisonment for adult females. Many were able to escape to other countries. Those remaining went into hiding. The unfolding catastrophe also attracted unprecedented prayer from around the world for hitherto hardened Afghanistan. With that, within months, despite all the Taliban threats and actions, 200 digital copies of the local language New Testament were reportedly being downloaded every day.

The foundations of a new move of God among the previously unreachable people, were being laid. In the most spiritually inhospitable environment imaginable, God was working in response to the prayers of His people. It has been well said that:

> God's is the power,
> Ours is the prayer,
> Without Him we cannot,
> Without us He will not.

Afghanistan is just one nation that has attracted media reporting for the first few decades of the 21st century. There are so many similar places ravaged by war, famine sickness, starvation, drought and corruption. If for no other reason, compassion should drive us to pray for them.

4. Compassion

When Paul Yonggi Cho was asked why so many people of his congregation went to Prayer Mountain to fast and pray, when they could have been spending their time doing other things, he replied:

> If you or members of your family were dying of cancer and you knew there was a cure, wouldn't you do whatever was necessary to produce healing? Many people are suffering from both physical and spiritual cancer. Material prosperity does not bring happiness and fulfillment. We have discovered that people's needs are met when we are totally dedicated to prayer and fasting.[26]

As we pray, things begin to happen. God unleashes His angels to intervene.

When Jesus saw the crowds of people flocking to hear Him teach or coming in the expectation of being healed from their sundry sicknesses, Matthew records, "He had compassion on them" (Matthew 9:36). With their needs in mind, He urged His disciples to pray.

As we pray, things begin to happen. God unleashes His angels to intervene. We read in 2 Kings 6 about hostile forces surrounding the city in which Elisha was residing. To allay fears, his servant's eyes were opened so that he could see "the hills full of horses and chariots of fire all around Elisha" (2 Kings 6:17).

Similarly, when the prayerful Daniel was locked up in a lions' den overnight, against all expectation no lion attacked him. Daniel explained the reason for such an unexpected outcome

---

26   Paul Y. Cho, *Prayer: Key to Revival*. Herts, England, Word Publishing, 1985, 14.

to a greatly relieved King Darius. "My God sent His angel and He shut the mouths of the lions" (Daniel 6:22).

In such cases, rather than our compassion motivating us to pray, it is more God's compassion, responding to the plight and prayer of His children. Either way, compassion causes the release of ministering angels to effect God's will.

In Nigeria in May 2018, 500 former Muslims gathered for a night meeting. They thought there was safety in numbers and the covering of darkness. They were mistaken. Boko Haram Islamists attacked capturing 72 men, women and children. In that they refused to deny their new faith and return to Islam, four of the men were killed.

To their wives an ultimatum was given. Return to Islam or watch while their children were killed. They were given overnight to consider their response. As the mothers wrestled with what response to make, some of the children reassured them that there was no cause for fear, because Jesus had visited them to tell them they would be protected from the killers.

The next morning the terrorists returned. They first lined up the children in front of a firing squad and then asked the mothers for their response. The mothers stated that they would not forsake Jesus, even though that meant their own lives and those of their children would be forfeited. Rifles were raised, readied to fire on command.

Suddenly members of the firing squad clutched their heads screaming, "Snakes are attacking us." A couple of them expired on the spot, while others dropped their rifles as all of them fled. Seizing the opportunity, a Christian darted forward, grabbed one of the

It is prayer, not our program which unleashes the power of God.

discarded rifles and was about to fire after the fleeing would be killers, when a child raced up and restrained him. The child said, "Don't shoot. Can't you see the men in white are fighting for us."[27]

Whenever people have been touched by the compassion of others praying for them or by God's compassion in responding to our prayers, two outcomes commonly result.

- We become aware that we have experienced something of the Kingdom of God "on earth as it is in heaven" (Luke 11:2).
- We ourselves are changed.

5. Experiencing the Kingdom

According to the record of historian Luke, when Jesus was being baptized, "As Jesus was praying heaven was opened, the Holy Spirit descended and a voice came from heaven saying, 'You are My Son whom I love' (Luke 3:21-22)".

Note it was as Jesus was praying that this remarkable event took place. It is prayer, not our program which unleashes the power of God.

Dwight Lyman Moody (1837-1899) was a well-known American evangelist. In 1872-1875 he visited the United Kingdom where he was warmly received. On one such occasion, after preaching at a church in London, he reported that as he preached, he had neither power nor liberty. He compared the experience to trying to pull a heavy train up a steep grade. He concluded that he was a fool to have consented to preach on this occasion. He therefore tried to be released from preaching in the same church that night. However, the pastor was insistent that Moody should preach as agreed.

---

27 *God's intervention saves 72 captive Nigerian Christians from Boko Haram firing squad.* Barnabas Aid, May/June 2019, 12.

As Moody fulfilled his obligation to preach, it seemed to him that all the powers of the unseen world had fallen upon the gathered congregation, which prevented his message cutting through. As quickly as possible he concluded his sermon. As he did so, to meet local expectations, he invited those who wished to accept Christ to stand. About 500 people stood up.

Moody thought they must have misunderstood him. He told them to sit down and explained again what the invitation was about. Then, instead of inviting them to respond by standing a second time, he told them to meet with the pastor in a nearby side room. So many tried to get into that room, that Moody again concluded there was still some mistake. He next gave instructions that, for any who really wanted to surrender their lives to Jesus, they were to return the following night.

Moody left for Ireland the following day. However, revival broke out in the church where he had preached. It then flowed out to other churches.

A question arose. What was the reason for the dramatic change between the apparent unresponsiveness in the morning service and the obvious moving of the Holy Spirit among the evening congregation? Moody himself later supplied the answer.

He discovered that there were two elderly sisters in the membership of the church. One of them was bedridden. The other heard Moody preach in the morning church service. She went home and roused her sister's curiosity with a question. "Who do you suppose preached for us this morning?"

"I don't know," replied the stay-at-home sister.

"Mr. Moody of Chicago was the preacher."

With that the bedridden sister exclaimed,

"What! Mr. Moody of Chicago! I've read of him in an American paper, and I have been praying God would send him to London and send him to our church. If I had known that he was to preach this morning I would have eaten no breakfast and I would have spent the whole morning in prayer and fasting. Now, sister, go out. Lock the door. Do not let anyone come to see me. Do not let them send me any dinner. I am going to spend the whole afternoon and evening in fasting and prayer!"[28]

And so, the power within the Kingdom of God was experienced by those in that service because one saint, although physically weak, was disciplined sufficiently to engage in prayer for all those present. If God could use the prayers of an elderly invalid to impact and change the lives of so many in a single meeting, what could he do with the rest of us able-bodied people if we also determined to prioritize prayer?

Reuben A. Torrey (1856-1928) accepted the invitation to become the Senior Minister after Moody relinquished that role at his church in Chicago. He was gratified to see that in his time, as in Moody's time, each Sunday the auditorium was packed. And each week, people continued to accept Jesus as their Lord and Savior.

The reason for this was not so much the preaching of Moody or Torrey. It was happening because of the people who stayed up late Saturday night or who rose early Sunday morning to pray for their pastor and his message. The same principle is found undergirding every servant of God whom the world might consider "great".

Charles Grandison Finney (1792-1875) was quite a different person from Moody or Torrey. He was greatly used of God to usher in a major revival through his work in the eastern United

---

28   R.A. Torrey, *The Power of Prayer.* Grand Rapids, Michigan, Zondervan, 1974, 37-38.

States. His preaching reshaped the nation. But behind his influential ministry, few discovered the real secret of his power.

An old man known as Father Nash arrived in each city in which Finney was to preach, a few weeks before the meetings were due to commence. He would rent a suitable room in which he stayed and prayed till Finney arrived. Finney's sermons packed a punch sufficient to bring the most hardened soul to repentance and conversion. By the conclusion of each series, Father Nash would have moved on to the site of the next series.

Nash had no home, no church support and often missed the nourishment of home-cooked meals. Finney, still today, is rightly acknowledged by historians for the effects of his ministry in his day. As for Nash, there was little or no public recognition for the part he played. But in the annals of heaven, his name will have been boldly recorded for the vital part he played in seeing 2.5 million people admitted into the Kingdom of Heaven. They experienced that Kingdom while still on earth, as they responded to the message Finney declared.[29]

Every would-be Finney needs a Nash—the more there are, the more effective that ministry will become.

6. Prayer Causing Change

a. In history

In May 1940, Adolph Hitler unleashed his troops against France and Belgium. Pulling back in the face of a superior and better-equipped German Army, the Allies quickly found themselves with nowhere else to go. At their backs was the English Channel. The German High Command boasted they would annihilate the trapped British Army. In England, Prime Minister Churchill prepared to announce that 300,000 of their soldiers had been captured or killed.

---

29   Wesley L. Duewel, *Touch the World Through Prayer*. Grand Rapids, Michigan, Francis Ashbury Press, 1986, 83–84.

Then, King George VI called for a National Day of Prayer. The British people responded by devoting themselves entirely to prayer during the appointed Day. Queues of people formed outside churches waiting to enter to join those packed inside who were already praying.

At the same time military commanders decided to attempt an evacuation. Lacking sufficient naval vessels to ferry the troops back to the safety of England, the call went out asking any who owned a vessel and who were willing to sail across the English Channel to bring home troops, to join in the Navy's rescue attempt. 800 vessels of all sizes set forth.

For reasons unknown even to Hitler's own generals, he ordered his army to halt their advance, thus denying them a certain momentous victory. For three days they stood down as the Allies worked frantically to effect the evacuation.

During the same period poor weather grounded the Luftwaffe. This enabled the troops to reach the beach to board the multiplicity of small boats to sail away across the Channel. And throughout the operation the sea remained remarkably calm.

Baffled historians, unable to fathom the power of prayer or unwilling to acknowledge its effectiveness, still refer to the extraordinary concurrence of events as "The Miracle of Dunkirk".

In World War II the last major offensive attempted by the AXIS powers on the Western Front, was known as the Battle of the Bulge (December 16, 1944–January 25, 1945). During the German Offensive through the Ardennes, 12,000 Allied soldiers were cut off and besieged at Bastogne in Belgium. An offer of surrender made by the Germans was rejected by US Brigadier General Anthony McAuliffe.

American General Patton's attempts to break through to rescue the troops was frustrated for a month by weather that rendered the attempt impossible. Patton calculated that all he needed to send in the Third Army to resupply and relieve the trapped troops was a window of just 24 hours of favorable weather. It never happened. With time running out to avert a disaster, Patton ordered his Third Army Chaplin, Colonel James O'Neill, to draft a prayer requesting a break in the weather to rescue the besieged troops.

The prayer read:

> Almighty and most merciful Father, we humbly beseech Thee, of Thy great goodness, to restrain these immoderate rains with which we have to contend. Grant us fair weather for battle. Graciously harken to us as soldiers who call upon Thee that, armed with Thy power, we may advance from victory to victory and crush the oppression and wickedness of our enemies and establish Thy justice among men and nations.

Printed on hundreds of thousands of cards it was distributed among the men of the Third Army.

The prayer worked. The weather cleared. Patton was able to smash through to reinforce and reequip the dwindling resources of the besieged troops in Bastogne. Chaplin O'Neill was awarded the Bronze Star. The citation declared it was "for writing a prayer". At least with hindsight, some acknowledgement was given to the Almighty's part in the victorious outcome.[30]

b. In others

Elder Kim went to see his pastor to seek his advice on an urgent and serious matter. He was trembling and ashen white. The problem was that to prepare for completing a major business deal, Mr. Kim had gone to his bank, withdrawn all his savings, locked them in his office safe and had slipped out for

---

30   *Dunkirk Evacuation* and *The Battle of the Bulge,* https://www.beliefnet.com/inspiration/3-times-prayer-changed-history.aspx (Viewed December 27, 2021).

lunch. Upon Kim's return he discovered a burglar had gained entry to his office, cracked open the safe and decamped with all his cash. Now, not only could he not complete the business deal, but he had no money to pay his employees' salaries. He was effectively bankrupt.

The pastor had no words of worldly wisdom. All he could recommend was that the devastated businessman go to the mountains to pray and fast for three days. Perhaps God would intervene.

On the third day Kim's wife at home received an urgent telephone call from a stranger wanting to speak with Kim as soon as possible. When the two men eventually met, the stranger advised Kim that he was the burglar who had stolen Kim's cash. All his life this fellow had lived by his ill-gotten gain from stealing from other people. Now he faced an unprecedented problem.

> "For three days I have tried to use your money, but every time when I reach out my hand, a spirit jumps out of your money and tries to kill me. I feel like I'm having a heart attack. I'm afraid. Will you please come and take away this money? I'm scared."

Mr. Kim advised the thief that the problem he was facing was because he, Kim, had been praying to God about the stolen cash and that the Holy Spirit had therefore been sent to protect the money. He further told the robber that he might well be killed unless he repented and accepted Jesus Christ as his savior. The burglar readily agreed. He repented and was baptized. The sinner now a saint, faithfully attended Kim's church.[31]

---

31   Unpublished untitled sermon delivered by Dr Paul Yonggi Cho, February 1, 1987.

c. In us

In September 2001, as my wife and I drove on a 2,000-kilometer interstate journey, I developed a severe headache. Shortly afterwards my vision was adversely affected. My wife took over and drove the rest of the way. Upon arrival at our destination, I immediately checked into a local medical clinic, some of whose staff were known personally to us. After a thorough examination, I was released and asked to return the next day for the results of some tests.

The next morning, I was advised that I "was healthier than a teenager."

However, when I went to drive the three kilometers back to our accommodation, I had lost sight again. When a little of it returned, I drove very slowly to where my wife was waiting for the news. When I tried to give her a report I couldn't speak.

By phone, the staff at the local clinic advised that we should proceed immediately to a specialist city hospital for further tests.

These showed that I had a spontaneous dissection of the carotid artery deep within my brain. Because of its location and size, no operation was possible. It was estimated I would live for about another three hours.

Having intermittently lost speech and sight, to make me as comfortable as possible, I was transferred to a quiet room on the 11th floor of the hospital. There I waited and waited—alone.

At 4:00am on the 12th day, the Lord woke me and told me to go to the bathroom. Although only three meters distant, that represented a significant if not dangerous distance as I had not moved during my hospitalization. Eventually having walked the three meters, I stared in disbelief, hardly able to recognize the thin, gaunt, unshaven face in the bathroom mirror.

Suddenly I was enveloped by the Holy Spirit. Filled with unspeakable joy and the love of the Lord, I started to sing, dance and to worship the Lord. Mindful of the physical danger of such exertions, I stopped and stood still. In the silence I received the Lord's message—"Today you will be released from this hospital. I have more work for you to do."

At 11:00am that same day, a neurologist informed me I was being released but I needed to stay close to the hospital in case…

After six weeks I was permitted to be driven the 2,000 kms back to my home city, there to check in to prearranged neurologists and ophthalmologists (my optic nerve had been damaged.)

For the next five years my progress was carefully monitored by medical specialists. Then came the last day. One of the medical specialists said, "With what happened to you, no one can explain why you are still alive. No one survives what you had. All the specialists in this building know of your case. We are agreed that your survival can only be described as a miracle."

I replied, "Doctor, allow me to tell you the secret of what happened. News of my predicament eventually reached the church of which I am the Senior Pastor. On the 11th night of my hospitalization, a special prayer meeting was called to pray for my complete recovery. Hundreds came and prayed for hours. I knew nothing of their prayer meeting. They knew nothing of the Lord's visitation to my room at 4:00am the next morning. During that night as the people prayed, without medical assistance, the healing process was accelerated."

To all this the Doctor replied, "As a medical professional I cannot comment on your explanation. However, I must warn you to be very careful. With what has happened you could drop dead without warning at any time."

Thanking the doctor for the advice, I replied that I had no intention of dying of rust as I rested permanently in a rocking chair. My life is in the Lord's hands as always. I will not die before I have completed every task He has for me to do.

This book, along with many others since then, is just one of the assignments the Lord has required of me.

Do I believe in prayer? Yes.

Does prayer work? Certainly.

Can it change history, others and us? Definitely.

I live life with short accounts. Every time I leave on another ministry trip and farewell my wife at the airport, we know we may never meet again on earth. I celebrate each extra day I'm given and work to the best of my ability. After all, this may be the last day I'm given to praise the Lord on earth and then…

So why should you pray? Apart from all else, there may come a day when your life also may depend on it!

Chapter 3
HEARING GOD

Prayer is not to hear oneself speak, but to arrive at silence and continue being silent; to wait till one hears God speak.

Søren Aabye Kierkegaard (1813–1855)

In the 1950s, as another of the periodic rounds of persecution oppressed Christians in China, Pastor Li in the southern province of Guandong was arrested. He was convicted of "counter-revolutionary activities" and sentenced to work in an iron ore mine in distant Heilongjiang in north-eastern China. His wife took their five children on the 3,200 km journey to live near where Pastor Li was imprisoned. She thought they would be able to see him occasionally. Pastor Li worked for 14 hours every day. Temperatures were way below zero. The limited amount of food he received was insufficient to keep him alive. After three months at the labor camp, he died.

To keep the family from also starving to death, the 12-year-old daughter visited the Director of the labor camp and begged for a job. The Director took sympathy on the family's plight and gave the girl the only job available. It was boring and paid very little. But even a little was better than nothing.

Every day 3,000 prisoners worked deep underground to extract the iron ore. At the surface near the entrance to the mine, all day the girl stood next to a red button. Should there be any danger down below, she would be advised. Her job was to press the button immediately. This would activate a warning signal throughout the mine. Everyone knew this was the signal to evacuate the mine urgently.

One afternoon as the girl stood ready at her station, she clearly heard someone order her to press the button. But when she turned to see who was giving the order, no one was present.

A short time later again the voice ordered her to press the button—quickly—now!

As she looked around once more, seeing no one, she wondered if it could be the Lord Himself speaking to her. But as before she hesitated to act.

With greater urgency a third time she was ordered to press the button. This time she acted. Shortly after the last worker came out of the mine, the earth shuddered as an earthquake destroyed the entire mine.

After it had been established that all 3,000 miners had been safely evacuated, the Director asked, "Comrade Li, how did you know to press the red button when you did?"

Li replied, "Jesus Christ told me... He loves you and has just demonstrated that by saving your lives. You must turn from your sins and give your lives to Him."

All 3,000 prisoners and the Director knelt and prayed to receive Jesus.[32]

Since the intimate relationship with our Creator was broken and lost through the disobedience of our progenitors at Eden, God Himself has launched innumerable initiatives to reconnect with us. Through many events, the Patriarchs, Prophets, Jesus and the Apostles, He has been unmistakably sending messages to us—if only we would listen.

---

32   Wolfgang Simon, Translator Steven Bufton. Friday-Fax Issue 43, Friday-fax@bufton. net, November 4, 2005.

Clearly it is to our advantage to be able to communicate with Him. And this should not be just a one-way stream of our most urgent needs. Such often occurs under the guise of prayer. We need to listen, to be ready to hear what God desires us to know. At times our very lives and those of others may depend upon it.

Millennia ago, through the Prophet Jeremiah, God declared, "Call to Me and I will answer you and tell you great and unsearchable things you do not know" (Jeremiah 33:3).

So how do we hear God?

1. Believe

The most fundamental precondition in being able to hear God, is to believe that He who spoke in the past still speaks today. Not only does He want to speak to other people, He wants to speak to us. There is ample evidence within the pages of the Bible as well as testimony of other saints, that He speaks.

Right at the beginning of human history we find God speaking to Adam (Genesis 2). He spoke to Noah (Genesis 6), giving him very specific instructions of what he was to do in view of an impending disaster that was much greater than that which the Chinese prisoners were helped to avoid.

He spoke to Moses conveying through him the entire law code by which future generations of His people were meant to live (Deuteronomy 1-31).

Then there was Samuel, the appointed king-maker and king-breaker (1 Samuel 3:2-10).

All the prophets heard Him speak (Isaiah 6:8-9; Jeremiah 1:4-5, 7-8). If God had not spoken, we would not have had any record of their words and ministries.

Supremely there was Jesus who testified, that He whom we call Father was speaking to Him, telling Him what to do day by day (John 5:30). After the high point of Jesus living among us, God continued to speak to Philip (Acts 8), Ananias (Acts 9), Peter and Cornelius (Acts 10), Paul (Acts 9), John (Revelation 1:9-11) and others.

This is precisely as Jesus said it would be:

> "...when He, the Spirit of truth comes He will guide you into all truth. He will not speak on His own; He will speak only what He hears, and He will tell you what is yet to come. He will bring glory to Me by taking what is Mine and making it known to you" (John 16:13-14).

A young man had attended a mid-week prayer and Bible study meeting at his church. The pastor had taught about how God speaks today. But the fellow still had a question in his mind. "Does God really speak to people today?" As he sat in his car readying himself to drive home it seemed natural to pray, "God, if you still speak, I am listening and will obey whatever you say."

As he drove down the main street of his town an odd thought popped into his mind, namely that he should buy a carton of milk. Could this be God? Without further confirmation he drove on. But again, the odd thought presented itself. Deciding on the off-chance it might be God, he went and bought the milk. But as he continued on his way home another unusual thought came to him—that he should turn and drive down Seventh Street.

After driving several blocks along Seventh Street the urge to stop came to him. It wasn't an area of town with which he was familiar. The poorly illuminated semi-industrialized area also left him feeling uncomfortable. Again, a strange urge came to him to cross the road to deliver the milk to a house that was shrouded in darkness. Perhaps all the people were away on holiday. In that case he wouldn't look too much of a fool. After all, who would know?

But if they were home and his door knocking woke them up to a stranger offering free milk… Somewhat timidly he approached the house, rang the bell and waited. Quickly lights came on. A not-too-friendly voice yelled out, "Who's there? Whadaya want?"

Before the would-be-milk deliveryman could make good his escape by disappearing into the darkened street, the door flung open. A menacing figure clothed only in jeans and T-shirt loomed above him. His glowering stare hardly seemed welcoming to the stranger on his doorstep at this hour of night.

Gallantly the young messenger thrust the milk into the householder's hands announcing it was a gift to whomever lived within. The man took the milk and without a further word, rushed back down the hallway shouting something in Spanish. Then down the same passageway came a woman followed by the man who was now carrying a crying baby. With tears streaming down his face the man explained, "We were praying as you rang our doorbell. We've had some big bills this month and we didn't have sufficient money to pay them all. Then we ran out of milk for the baby. We were just asking God to help us get some milk somehow."

The wife chipped in, "I asked God to send an angel with some milk. Are you an angel?"

With that the milk delivery man became a cashier. He took out his wallet and handed over all the money he had. He figured it was well worth it to start to learn how exciting it can be to hear and obey God's

If we believe, we too should expect to hear something from God.

voice.[33] After all, young Samuel had to learn by trial and error. And look what he ended up becoming once he learned to expect God to speak (1 Samuel 3).

If we believe, we too should expect to hear something from God.

2. Expect

Georg Müller (1805–1898) established the Ashley Down orphanage in Bristol, England. During his lifetime he was responsible for caring for 10,000 orphans. He never made any public appeals for support. But he prayed urgently and often. On one occasion as the 300 children resident in the orphanage were dressed and ready for school, the orphanage matron advised Müller that the children had not eaten breakfast and worse still there was no food to give them.

Müller instructed that all the children should be seated in the dining hall, after which he thanked God for the food and waited. Within minutes a baker arrived and advised Müller that during the night he'd been unable to sleep. He realized the orphanage would need bread, so he got up and baked three additional batches that he was now delivering.

Shortly after this a milkman was at the door. His cart had broken down outside the orphanage. Rather than have the milk ruined before the cart could be fixed (there was no refrigeration), he offered all his milk for the 300 children waiting inside.[34]

Later in life, as Müller was travelling by ship to Canada to fulfill a speaking engagement, a dense fog settled upon the ocean. Having no such a device as radar, the ship slowed

---

33   Anonymous, *Prepare to Fly*. http://www.mountainwings.com (Viewed March 26, 2003).
34   George Müller, *Orphanages Built by Prayer*. https://www.christianity.com/church/church-history/church-history-for-kids/george-mueller-orphanages-built-by-prayer-11634869.html (viewed January 4, 2022).

almost to a standstill, to avoid the possibility of collision with other vessels or Titanic-destroying icebergs.

Müller went to the captain and asked him to resume full speed lest he arrive late

It is in the silence of the heart that God speaks.

for his engagement. The captain responded, that under the circumstances, he could not grant the request. Müller remonstrated that, in 40 years of Christian ministry, he had never once been late for an appointment. The captain remained unmoved.

So Müller then invited the captain to join him in prayer that God might disperse the fog. As they knelt, Müller told the captain not to pray because he did not believe in what they were doing. After Müller prayed and they went outside onto the deck, the captain was astonished to see that the fog had dissipated. It was no surprise to Müller. It was exactly as he expected it to be.

3. Listen

Our ability to listen for whatever God may want to say to us, is made easier or more difficult depending upon our environment. Obviously, we make things easier for ourselves if we follow the example of Jesus. He often left behind the noise of a multiplicity of voices and went to where He could be alone. That may be locked away in some convenient room (Matthew 6:6) or beyond the cacophony of urban sprawl (Matthew 14:23).

It was when they were alone that God was able to get through to Moses (Exodus 19), Elijah (1 Kings 19), Paul (Galatians 1:15-17) and many others. It is when we are alone that we can start to quiet down, to be still (Psalm 37:7) and wait expectantly for God to speak (Psalm 130:5). In the stillness we get to know who it is who desires to speak with us (Psalm 46:10).

Mother Teresa (1910-1997), founder of the Sisters of Charity order, said in 1989, "I always begin my prayer in silence. It is in the silence of the heart that God speaks. We need to listen because it's not what we say but what He says to and through us that matters."[35]

In adopting this approach, she was following wise advice given by Solomon three millennia earlier. He said, "Do not be quick with your mouth. Do not be hasty in your heart to utter anything before God. God is in heaven and you are on earth, so let your words be few" (Ecclesiastes 5:2).

A native American proverb expresses it more succinctly, "Listen or your tongue will keep you deaf."

So often in church meetings we pray, "Speak, Lord, for your servants are listening." Then we wonder why we may not hear anything from God. We were created with one mouth and two ears. It's a good reminder that we should listen more than we speak.

Some years ago, a shipping company sought to employ a wireless operator. Prospective applicants were notified to report for a job interview on a particular day at a given place and time. At the specified time the waiting room was buzzing with the chatter of the job hopefuls. So engrossed were they in conversation with one another that all except one person failed to hear a message in Morse code. It was coming through a loudspeaker hanging in a corner of the waiting room.

That one exception arose and walked through the doorway to the inner office. Shortly afterwards he emerged and told the rest he had been given the job. They were unimpressed. After all, many of them had arrived earlier than this fellow. They hadn't even been given the courtesy of an interview to showcase their skills. But in one critical area they had already

---

35 *Something Beautiful for God*. Time, September 15, 1997, 73.

failed a test that ruled them out as unsuitable for the job. They had failed to listen.

While they had been preoccupied with their chatter, a message in Morse code had been broadcast over the speaker. It informed any who were attentive, that the first person to follow the directions being broadcast who entered the inner office, would become the successful applicant.

> **Other books give us information. The Bible causes our transformation.**

Only as we listen will we hear and learn.

God is so desirous to communicate clearly with us that He has provided some well-tested hearing aids.

4. Hearing Aids

a. The Bible

The most time-tested reliable aid prepared for us is the Bible. Other books give us information. The Bible causes our transformation. It tells us who we are, how we got here, why we are here and depending upon decisions we make, where we are going in the future vastness of eternity.

When English monarchs ascend the throne, at a certain point during the coronation ceremony, the presiding Archbishop will say, "We present you with the Book, the most valuable thing that this world affords. Here is wisdom: this is the royal Law; these are the lively Oracles of God."

Similar advice used to be observed in the United States of America. Former President Woodrow Wilson once said,

> I ask of every man and woman in this audience that from this night on they will realize that part of the destiny of America lies in their daily perusal of this great book of

revelations–that if they would see America free and pure they will make their own spirits free and pure by this baptism of the Holy Scripture.

The Psalmist said, "Your word is a lamp to my feet and a light for my path" (Psalm 119:105).

When we are in the dark, nothing is more valuable than a light. The lamp that is mentioned here was a small oil lamp. The light from its lighted wick was insufficient to see what was beyond the bend in the road or where the next hill may be. But it gave sufficient light to show the next immediate step. After all that's all we need to see.

However, the Bible is not an ordinary lamp. "The lamp of the Lord searches the spirit of a man; it searches out his inmost being" (Proverbs 20:27). As we read the Bible, it reads us and informs us of changes we need to make in our own lives and the directions we are to take. We are advised to "meditate on it day and night… to be careful to do everything written in it. Then (we) will be prosperous and successful" (Joshua 1:8).

As we meditate on what we read in the Bible, the Holy Spirit often highlights verses from which other thoughts arise as spontaneous impressions.

This is the second way God uses to speak to us.

b. Spontaneous Impressions

"…You teach me wisdom in the inmost place" (Psalm 51:6).

Rees Howells (1879-1950) was a great man of prayer. On one occasion he and his wife were to embark on a ship that would take them to where they had been appointed to work in Africa, with the South Africa General Mission. But first they faced a test of faith–the challenge of getting to London by train. They had prayed asking the Lord for money for the train fare, but none had come. They had only enough funds to travel part of the distance to Llanelli. There they would change trains to continue their journey to London. At least they were able to complete that part of their journey. As they waited on the station, they prayed that the Lord would somehow provide money to buy the tickets for the remainder of the journey.

Then the Holy Spirit impressed upon Howells, that if he had the money wouldn't he get into the queue outside the ticket office to buy the tickets before the train arrived? Howells agreed and obeyed. There were about 12 other passengers in front of them buying their tickets. Slowly it was coming close for Howells' turn to buy tickets at the window.

When there were only two others between him and the window, a man stepped out of the crowd. He had come to farewell the African bound missionaries. He apologized that he couldn't wait longer because he had to depart to open his shop. But as he left, he pressed 30 shillings into Rees Howells' hand, sufficient to buy the train tickets to London.[36]

He had learned to recognize God's voice through spontaneous impressions that came to him through the Holy Spirit. Like Abraham before him, "… he did not waver through unbelief regarding the promise(s) of God but was strengthened in his faith and gave glory to God, being fully persuaded that God had power to do what He had promised" (Romans 4:20–21).

c. Dreams and Visions

Dreams are those that occur while we sleep. Visions are "seen" while we are awake. Within the Bible, there are many examples of God using these methods to bypass our consciousness, to tell us something He considers we need to know. Specifically, God spoke through dreams and visions to prophets, to whom He imparted divine revelations (Numbers 12:6, Hosea 12:10).

---

36   Norman Grubb, *Rees Howells Intercessor*. London, Lutterworth Press, 1962, 156–157.

Anyone who has read the Bible can't help but remember the vivid dreams of Joseph (Genesis 37), Daniel (Daniel 7) or the vision of Ezekiel (Ezekiel 37). The outcomes from these events were critical to the life of the nation. Later through the prophet Joel, we learn that dreams and visions were to become a much more common experience among believers (Joel 2:28). They would no longer be the exclusive province of selected political or religious leaders.

Regardless of our reluctance in materialistically dominated Western society to consider this possibility, in developing countries reports of dreams and visions are far more common. They are accepted as a legitimate means of God speaking to us—provided there is nothing in them contrary to the will of God as revealed in the Bible.

In December 1991, God spoke in dreams and visions to 24 Muslim leaders along the Bulgarian-Turkish border. Initially none knew that a similar message had been communicated to each of the other 23 in a similar way. What they saw and heard was a person saying to each, "I am Jesus, the Messiah. You must repent of your sins and put your faith in Me to be forgiven. God has sent Me to turn you from error to truth. You must go to (your) mosque and proclaim this to the people."

When they obeyed what they had heard and shared the message with their people, each began to repent and to seek God. When they did, as in Acts 2, they were filled with the Holy Spirit and began to speak in languages unknown to them. In February 1992 two of their number journeyed to the capital city of Sofia seeking Bibles and help to understand what had happened.[37]

Seven years later Bill Bright, the founder of Campus Crusade reported,

---

[37] Raymond C. Perkins Jr., *Prayer for Israel*, New Zealand, Number 71, July–August 1993, 1-2.

"Never before in history has God moved so supernaturally to draw millions of Muslims to Himself throughout the world... (Our) office has received thousands of letters from Muslims. Many tell of a dream they had in which Jesus declared, 'I am the way.'"[38]

In obedience we take up an issue in prayer until there is a release followed by peace.

By 2015, researchers were estimating that in recent decades the number of Muslim Background Believers (MBBs) had reached 10 million.[39] While the data was questioned, there was agreement that an unprecedented movement was underway.[40] Many of these new believers had been impacted by dreams and visions. This is because "dreams are the only means... by which the average Muslim expects to hear directly from God."[41]

Male adult Muslims leave Islam on pain of death. Given our normal preference for life over death, this means it is almost impossible for Muslims to follow Jesus of the Gospels. Only those who can see the invisible do the impossible. When God speaks through dreams and visions, such is the gripping power of these encounters, that Muslims are leaving their former faith to follow Jesus even though that will cost them everything—perhaps even their lives. But that after all is what Jesus said it would cost to be one of His disciples (Matthew 10:16–23).

38 World Revival News, *Revival World Report*. July/August 1999, 13.
39 Duane Alexander Miller and Patrick Johnston, *Believers in Christ from a Muslim Background: A Global Census*. Interdisciplinary Journal of Research on Religion, Vol. II, Article 10, 2015.
40 Gene Daniels, *How Exactly Do We Know What We Know about Kingdom Movements?* In Warrick Farah, Ed., *Motus Dei, The Movement of God to Disciple the Nations*. Littleton, CO., USA, William Carey Publishing, 2021, 58–60.
41 Nabeel Qureshi, *Seeking Allah, Finding Jesus*. Grand Rapids, Michigan, Zondervan, 2014.

d. Release and Peace

A fourth element involved in hearing God is through release and peace. This occurs when in obedience we take up an issue in prayer and continue interceding until there is a release from the compulsion to pray, followed by peace. In this way we know that the matter is settled in heaven and eventually we will see the outcome on earth.

In September 1943 during World War II, a critical battle was commencing. The Allied forces were attempting to land troops and armaments at Salerno in Italy. If they could secure the beach and go on to capture the strategic heights above, from there they could fight their way south to capture Rome. The strategic plans were a well-kept military secret.

At the Bible College of Derwen Fawr in Swansea, Wales, an evening prayer meeting concluded. But at 9:45pm staff and students gathered again. The Director made a solemn announcement, "The Lord has burdened me between the meetings with the invasion at Salerno. I believe our men are in great difficulties and the Lord has told me that unless we can pray through, they are in danger of losing their hold."

There had been no official news in the media as to what might be happening, but immediately the group commenced to pray intensely for victory and deliverance of the Allied forces. This continued till they suddenly found themselves "praising and rejoicing, believing that God had heard and answered." At exactly 11:00pm, they rose from their knees and began to sing and thank God for the victory. The matter had been settled in heaven.

The midnight radio news mentioned the gravity of the situation in Salerno and that unless there was a miracle, the beachhead would be lost before the morning. It was days later when a newspaper report revealed what became known as, "The Miracle of Salerno".

As the troops were attempting to land, they came under intense artillery fire. There was no way in which they could reach their primary objective. Suddenly for no reason, all firing from the well-entrenched German positions ceased. In deathly silence and breathless anticipation, the Allied troops waited for it to resume. It never did. Throughout the night an effective landing operation was executed that enabled the beachhead to be secured as a base, from which the troops were later to advance and capture Rome.

The time when all AXIS firing stopped–11:00pm![42]

e. Through Others

A fifth way God frequently speaks to those who will listen, is through other trusted believers. As believers we are not meant to live in isolated silos. We are part of a community called the church. Within that body there will be always spiritually sensitive, mature believers, who do hear God and who are willing to pass on what they believe they hear, if they know we are willing to receive what they say.

The wisest man who ever lived, King Solomon of Israel, knew the value of listening to godly advice (Proverbs 12:15; 19:20). He also highlighted the danger of not receiving such advice (Proverbs 17:10).

I personally can testify that I might not have stepped aside from my chosen profession as a psychologist to start training for the Christian ministry, had it not been for a godly leader in our church. He pointed out to me that the giftings God had given me were not just to pursue a career with excellent financial prospects. What I had received was to be used to expand and strengthen the Kingdom of God.

After this redirection, I would never have considered anything but ministry in my own country, had not another

---

42   Grubb, 262-264.

> **The most important element in the process of hearing God is that we obey whatever He says.**

friend challenged me. He said that God had told him that I was to take his place as a cross-cultural worker. It was in one of the world's poorest countries. It was to be among a people who, despite two centuries of missionary work there, had made virtually no response to the gospel from among them.

I accepted that challenge and started training to relocate to another country. I was so intent on following God's call as I knew it, that I would never have discovered the woman I was to marry, had it not been for another godly leader in my home church. He identified for me whom he believed was the chosen one with whom I was to share life. (As I write, today is our 54th wedding anniversary!)

Then, in our work among this most difficult to reach people, God revealed to us a totally different way of working. This resulted in historically unprecedented response. We would never have left this assignment for the remainder of our lives, had not God used other people to call us back to our home country to found a different sort of church. It became one of the largest in the nation.

The Kingdom rewards can be great if we listen to what God says to us through trusted others. Having heard is one thing. How we respond is equally important.

5. Response
Our response includes two steps.

a. Write it Down
To the prophet Habakkuk God said: "Write down the revelation and make it plain on tablets" (Habakkuk 2:2).

When the Apostle John received a revelation from God, he also wrote it down (Revelation 1:3, 11).

Our contemporary equivalent would be to capture the message on our cell phones, tap it into our laptops or secure it on a memory stick. The critical factor is not to lose what we think God might be saying to us. Without keeping a record, we too easily forget what was said, as life moves us on to the next event and the next and the next.

However, the most important element in the process of hearing God is that we obey or implement whatever He says.

b. Obey

Jesus repeatedly emphasized that it is through obedience that we demonstrate our love for Him (John 14:15, 21, 23; 15:10). The Apostle John, by his life and words, repeatedly reaffirmed this principle (1 John 5:3; 2 John 6).

God is unlikely to speak to us if He knows we have no intention of doing what He asks of us. Once Saul was first dramatically confronted by Jesus, through a vision (Acts 9:1-9), ever after he obeyed whatever was required of him. Much later in life, renamed Paul, he could testify before King Agrippa, "I was not disobedient to the vision from heaven" (Acts 26:19). Even if at times this was against his own will (Acts 16:6-7), he chose to be guided by a new vision to preach elsewhere (Acts 16:9-10).

No matter how God chooses to communicate, the only acceptable response to what He may be requiring of us, is total immediate obedience. Partial obedience, selective obedience, delayed obedience, is all disobedience. Even though we might be unsure how to complete the assignment, as we take the first tentative step of obedience, we can be certain that what He ordains He sustains. Also, the results are often far more spectacular than what we could imagine, compared to carefully controlled well-planned, adequately resourced human efforts.

A pastor had shown visiting church dignitaries something of the vitality of local church life. Finally, he wanted them to meet two young women who were church planters. They had both become Christians while listening to radio broadcasts. They felt that God was also calling them to become missionaries. However, their pastor had tried to persuade them to remain in their local church to learn how to witness to others first.

The young ladies insisted that, according to the Bible they had been given, Jesus' command was to go. The pastor next pointed out that they were very young and had only come to know Jesus six months previously. In various ways the pastor tried to dissuade the women from going. Eventually he agreed to their request and assigned them to locate to Hainan Island off the coast of mainland China. The island was inhabited by fishing communities.

There had been little or no communication between the young ladies and their pastor for two years. As they had returned to the city to replenish their supply of Bibles and other literature, the Pastor asked them to meet with him and the visiting foreigners. The meeting was to take place in a well-appointed hotel suitable to foreign tastes.

As the pastor waited in the foyer, he noticed the immaculately uniformed hotel staff were preventing two people from entering. Understandably, this was hardly an acceptable place to allow peasants dressed in black pajamas and broad-brimmed bamboo fishermen's hats. The pastor suddenly realized that these were the missionaries for whom they had been waiting.

Quickly he intervened and escorted the young women to a room where they could talk privately. After an exchange of introductory pleasantries, the visitors enquired as to whether the ladies had been able to commence any church on Hainan.

Apologetically the ladies pointed out, that in that they had been on the island only two years, not many churches had been started.

"How many?"

"Not many… The people were not very friendly… They became very vicious (and) told us they were going to drown us in the ocean."

"How many churches?"

"Only thirteen."

"Thirteen!"

"No… Thirty."

"How many people are in the churches?"

"Not many… not many."

"How many?"

"Two hundred and twenty… Not many."

"Two hundred and twenty in 30 churches?"

"Oh no. That is only one small church."

"How many in the big churches?"

"Not many."

"Please, ladies, how many?"

"Only four thousand nine hundred. We have just started."

"How did you do this?"

"We did nothing. We just prayed."

"What else did you do?"

"After we prayed the Holy Spirit would tell us what to do... We would do it and kept praying."

They just prayed and obeyed.

God's work done in God's way by those who will believe, expect, listen and obey, will always attract the supernatural blessing of God.[43]

Remember, this is God who consistently identifies as I AM (Exodus 3:14; John 8:58). Not I WAS or I SHALL BE, but I AM. He is the ever-present one. Just as He spoke in former times, He still does so today.

Even so, a question remains to trouble us. How can we be certain that it is God who is trying to speak to us?

---

43 Carl Lawrence, *The Coming Influence of China*. Gresham, OR, USA, Vision House Publishing, 1996, 186–192.

Chapter 4
INCREASING CERTAINTY

All my requests are lost in one Father,
on earth Thy will be done.

Charles Wesley (1707-1788)

A railway inspector began checking tickets on a morning train. He discovered that the first passenger he checked had the wrong ticket. He advised the passenger that he would have to change trains at the next station.

As he moved through the train checking tickets at random, he was surprised to find numbers of other passengers were also holding the wrong tickets. How could so many of them have made the same mistake? Suddenly it dawned upon him. It was not they who were on the wrong train. It was him![44]

How often have we taken a certain course of action believing we were within the will of God, only later to discover to our embarrassment that we were mistaken? If "the ultimate end and the supreme motive for each Christian is the will of God,"[45] the challenge is how do we know with any degree of certainty, that we have heard God correctly?

Without oversimplifying a potentially complex matter, there are a few principles we can follow to minimize mistakes and maximize certainty. These provide a road map along which

---

44   Warren Wiersbe, *Confident Living*. Good News Broadcasting Association Inc., 1998.
45   Harold Lindsell, *An Evangelical Theology of Missions*. Grand Rapids, Michigan, Zondervan, 1970.

to progress. They give us increased confidence that we have heard God and are on the right track in following His will.

The first of these is the most difficult to implement.

1. Stop wanting your own will

So often when we pray and seek God's will rather than just report for duty, we tend to want to give God our instructions. We might already have a fair idea of what He requires of us, but to our way of thinking that seems too difficult or too dangerous. So like Moses (Exodus 3), Gideon (Judges 6), Isaiah (Isaiah 6) or Jeremiah (Jeremiah 1) we produce many excuses as to why it couldn't be us. In so doing we forget that:

- God doesn't so much call the qualified. He qualifies the called.
- The will of God will never lead us to where the grace of God will not protect us.
- The safest place to be is in the center of God's will.

The Apostle Paul encouraged believers in Rome to understand that if they really wanted to know what God's will for their lives was, then the first prerequisite was that they totally surrender even their own bodies to God and thenceforth exist as living sacrifices. As they set aside their wills, they would discover God's will (Romans 12:1-2).

Temple Gairdner (1873-1928), a Church Missionary Society (CMS) worker in Cairo, Egypt, understood the principle well. It's reflected in his written prayers:

> O God, You know that I do not want anything else
> but to serve You and men.
> Always, all of my life.

Toward the end of his life, he wrote:

> Lord, I am willing to appear to the world

and to all to have lost my life if only
I may have made it good in Your sight.

Dying to self is never easy. It's very counter-cultural in societies that preach we are to look out for number one—ourselves.

Success is a greasy pole, mounted only by climbing over the backs of others who may be trying to be top dog in some corporation, to occupy the glass office in the corner of the highest floor in the building, to have a specially reserved executive car park spot or better still, an exclusive elevator to whisk the successful ones aloft to their executive suites. In Western societies we have so many ways to vaunt our shallow temporary successes.

The church is not immune from such distractions. In some denominations clergy accumulate titles and special robes to indicate promotions. Others who lack a liturgical ladder measure success by the size and location of their congregations. Rare would it be for a well-known urban or city pastor to resign their charge to accept responsibility in some far-off rural location.

We know that Jesus equated fruitfulness with being like "a kernel of wheat (that) falls into the ground and dies" (John 12:24). We admire that principle being implemented in the lives of others. But when it becomes our turn, having fallen "into the ground", before long we complain it's too dark, too cold, too lonely and we want to get out into the warm sunshine again. We may do so, but according to Jesus' analogy that is achieved at the cost of future potential fruitfulness.

In Muslim practice, at one of their annual Eid festivals, to demonstrate costly sacrificial intent, each household is required to slaughter an animal as an act of obtaining forgiveness of sins since the last sacrifice was offered. Poorer people may be able to offer a chicken. More wealthy people often engage in an unspoken competition with their neighbors to see who has the most outstanding costly animal.

At the appointed time, the animals are led to a visible roadside place adjacent to the owner's house. Burly males using ropes next attempt to force the animal on to its side on the ground. After this, its throat will be cut by the householder using a very sharp knife. The blood of this sacrifice will be collected in a bowl.

However, what sometimes happens is that during the pre-slaughter procedures, the sacrificial animal realizes that what is about to happen may not be in its own best interests. It commences to struggle violently. In some cases, it escapes with the would-be slaughterers in hot pursuit. In so doing the animal has voided the fundamental purpose of its central position on the big day. It's no longer the sacrificial animal upon which every other ceremony and prayer on the day depended.

So often we also are like those runaway animals. In obedience and humility, we start well. But for various reasons, when things are not quite to our liking, we break free of those commitments that bind us to the cross of Christ and flee to another assignment more favorable to our future fortune. As a "sacrificial animal" we are to lie down, live dead and stay dead until our Master redirects otherwise. That's what Jesus implied when He urged His disciples to take up their cross (Luke 9:23).

"Islam" means *submission*. Muslims are those who see themselves as slaves, submitted to the will of Allah, following teaching revealed through their Prophet Mohammad. When Muslims discover Jesus, while they obtain freedom from the shackles of Sharia Law, they never resile from that basic attitude of submission now to teaching within the Bible and allowing God to guide how He will. They know that in the end this is best. "Mustapha" expressed it well when he wrote:

> O God,
> I am Mustapha the tailor
> And I work at the shop of Mohammed Ali.

The whole day I sit
And pull needle and thread through cloth,
O God,
You are the needle and I am the thread.
I am attached to You and I follow You.
When the thread tries to slip away from the needle
It becomes tangled up and must be cut
So that it can be put back in the right place.
O God,
Help me to follow You whenever You lead.
For I am only Mustapha the tailor
And I work at the shop of Mohammed Ali.[46]

To stop wanting our own way is fundamental to all that follows. The second principle is to look into the Word of God.

2. Look Into the Bible

God's Word reveals to us His will. If we are unable to find reference in the Bible to the thing we might be praying about, then possibly we shouldn't even be praying for it. God's Word and His will never change. "The entrance of Your words gives light. It gives understanding to the simple" (Psalm 119:130).

It's one thing to be told something by the Holy Spirit by having verses of Scripture highlighted, or a trusted mature godly person sharing a helpful insight. It's quite another to listen, receive and act upon such insights.

It's vital that we find God's guidance based upon His Word.

As we lurch through the miasma of our uncertainties, we need to discover clarity according to God's Word. "…Give me understanding according to Your word" (Psalm 119:169).

46   Stuart Robinson, *Prayer.* Blackburn Baptist Church Bulletin, October 23, 1988, 1.

It's vital that we find God's guidance based upon His Word, rather than resort to any lesser authority, even though that other might seem more attractive at the time. The Psalmist expressed it thus:

"Turn my heart toward Your statues and not toward selfish gain. Turn my eyes away from worthless things; renew my life according to Your Word" (Psalm 119:36-37).

One of the biggest decisions we ever make in life is whom we will marry. As a new believer I wanted to marry only the woman of God's choice for me. I believed He would know far better than I could who would be the best partner for me for the whole of life. Given the increasing number of failed marriages ending in divorce, I desperately didn't want to add to their number. So, in my newfound faith I commenced to pray. But I had a problem. As an athlete and captain of a football team, I had no difficulty in attracting girls who wanted to be dated by me.

As I prayed, I asked God to keep me pure for the woman of His choice and to do likewise for the one He had chosen for me. Behavioral characteristics helped me to eliminate a few from my list of possible prospects. In one case the young lady was so aggressive in her intent to fulfill her desires that, like Joseph, I literally ran and made good my escape.

To lessen the possibility of falling into temptation, I stopped altogether having any association with the opposite sex. Every night my last prayer of the day was for the woman of God's choice for me. Of course, I had fixed in my mind the image of the woman God was reserving for me. Unsurprisingly it coincided with one of the Hollywood bombshells of that era. The years ticked by as I patiently waited until, as I have mentioned elsewhere, a leader in my home church named for me the woman whom he thought was God's choice. She had been in our church all the time and I had not even noticed her.

Part of my problem was I was ignorant of much of what the Bible has to say on the matter. Had I been aware of Proverbs 31:10-31 that would have eliminated 99.5% of the women I had been considering. All the time here was one who ticked every box listed in Proverbs

> **Prayer is simply a two-way conversation between you and God.**

31. As I prayed with new understanding, quickly I realized this woman could be the one. The question was would she agree with my discernment.

Within weeks I proposed marriage to her but warned her she needed to take several months to pray about this because God had a call upon my life. I could therefore never know what our future circumstances together would be. I was prepared to go anywhere and do anything. Our life could be precariously absent of all the financial and other securities people normally build together. Months later came the night when I asked for her reply. Her answer?

"You are either dumb or slow witted. I knew over a year ago God had selected you to be my husband. Since then, I've just been praying for you and waiting for the Lord to open your eyes!"

Through prayer and her own Bible study, she had discerned God's will. He had given a promise. Faith believed it. Hope anticipated it while patience quietly waited for it to come to pass.

3. Listen

The great well-known trusted evangelist of the 20th century was Billy Graham. He is frequently quoted as saying, "Prayer is simply a two-way conversation between you and God." This implies that while either one speaks the other listens.

Jesus confirmed the concept when He said, "My sheep listen to My voice" (John 10:27).

A thousand years before the arrival of Jesus on earth, through King David, God Himself promised, "I will instruct you and tech you in the way you should go; I will counsel you and watch over you" (Psalm 32:8).

Both Father and Son confirm that we humans have a capacity to hear when they speak. All Christians accept that God speaks through the Bible. But many in our science-conditioned materialist West would have trouble in believing that God still speaks today in addition to the Scriptures. In this they interpret the Bible through their experience—or lack of it. Rather we need to interpret our experience through the Bible. Nowhere does it say that God would cease communication with us once the canon of Scripture was determined.

Jesus encouraged His disciples to believe that when they were facing a difficult situation, they should not be worried because the Holy Spirit would tell them what to say (Matthew 10:19-20). Again, God speaks and comes to our aid if we will listen.

God created us with an ability to shut our mouths but with ears that always remain open. We ought to heed the clue and give closer attention to listening than talking. At a human level we can win more friends by listening, using our ears, than we can with our mouths that are always talking.

Abraham was given the exalted title of being a "friend of God" (2 Chronicles 20:7). Perhaps he was so described because he developed his listening capacity and acted upon what God said to him, even if that meant potentially the death of his own son, Isaac (Genesis 22:1-19).

Sister Chang was the leader of a house church in Henan Province in China. She claimed that while she was praying, she heard God tell her to preach about her Christian faith on the steps of the local police station. Within minutes of her starting to preach she was arrested and jailed. But in jail she continued to preach to a captive congregation. The result was that within three months 800 women had decided to follow Jesus. This transformed the whole atmosphere within the jail.

The Director of the jail was so impressed he offered Chang her freedom. He also offered her a job paying for the time, an astonishing salary of 3,000 Yuan (US$375) per month. Included in the offer was a chauffeur-driven car and a spacious apartment.

Chang did not accept the offer. As she said to the Director, "Jesus has been wonderful to me since I've known him. I don't think the offer of a salary, car and chauffeur match His plans for my life. I belong to Jesus alone and I want to preach the good news."[47]

Our fruitfulness and productivity in God's Kingdom, directly correlates with our ability to listen, hear and act in accordance with what He is saying to us.

4. Test

A fourth principle to use to increase certainty in discerning what God may be requiring of us is the test of circumstance. In so doing however, we need to remember always that we are by nature somewhat egocentric. That being so, we therefore have an innate tendency to interpret circumstances in terms of our own comfort, desires and self-interest.

Should the prophet Jonah be the guest speaker at some Christian function, if we remained unaware of the back story of his life, he could present a riveting testimony. He could commence by recounting how he just happened to be walking along the wharves watching the ships loading and unloading their cargos, when he just happened to strike up a conversation

---

47   Grahame Orpin, *World Outreach*. January 6, 2004.

with a ship's captain, who advised him he would be shortly casting off as soon as he could fill the last available berth he had for a paying passenger.

Upon enquiry by Jonah, the captain would have advised the cost of a below-deck berth, which as luck would have it, Jonah just happened to have the right amount of money to pay for that berth. So, he paid up, boarded ship and sailed away on a course set in a southwesterly direction.

All that is "coincidentally" just fine. Here was a man in the right place at the right time, with the right amount of money to secure passage, right in the direction he wanted to go. What a chain of events! How good that all the circumstances meshed perfectly together, if only...

If only we didn't know that God had directed him to travel, not southwest to run away but northeast to Nineveh where God had an assignment for him.

In my work in many developing countries, I've often noticed how many missionaries from developed Western nations feel called to work in developing countries only in those places where there is electricity, air-conditioning and appropriate schools for their children. In the meantime, out in the rural areas where most of the unreached population lives, they remain unreached.

Some years ago, I sat with a woman who told me how God had told her she was in effect to divorce her husband and marry another man. All three were practicing Christians, members in standing of a local church. She even produced verses from the Bible to support her anticipated course of action. She was not interested to learn she was misinterpreting Scripture by lifting verses out of context. Nor would she listen to what God had clearly spelled out elsewhere in the Bible about marriage, divorce and adultery. She was wholly misguided by her feelings and through that lens misinterpreted everything to satiate her own desires.

Misinterpreting circumstances is relatively common. Joshua 9 records how Gibeonites arrived in the Israelite camp decked out as if they had travelled from afar and pitched a good yarn to support the deception of their appearance. In so doing they were seeking a way out of conflict. They were living immediately adjacent to the Israelites. Their ruse worked initially because the Israelites looked only at the circumstances presented to them. They failed to seek the counsel of God.

> **When God is the object of our trust the Bible refers to this as faith.**

An equivalent repetition of the event of Gideon's fleeces in Judges 6, as confirmation of God's guidance, is often resorted to by Christians. It certainly is an amazing story of how God patiently encouraged young Gideon. The principle is valid–but never, unless there is more than an appeal to circumstance, as the sole indicator of what God is saying.

Ultimately no matter how many principles we deploy in our search for certainty, we are going to have to take a step of faith and trust.

5. Trust

Trust involves letting go and believing God will catch you. When God is the object of our trust the Bible refers to this as faith.

"The righteous will live by faith" (Habakkuk 2:4: Romans 1:17). "We live by faith not by sight" (2 Corinthians 5:7).

We might dream up one thousand ways that according to our reckoning might please God. But without faith none will (Hebrews 11:6).

Jesus said, "Everything is possible to him who believes" (Mark 10:27). Jesus further assured us that we don't have to be giants in the field of faith to see God working through us to achieve amazing outcomes.

"I tell you the truth, if you have faith as small as a mustard seed, you can say to this mountain, 'Move from here to there and it will move.' Nothing will be impossible for you" (Matthew 17:20).

In 979, in the newly established city of Cairo in Egypt, Caliph Al-Mu'iz Li Din Illah Al-Fatimi invited Christians and Jews to debate their respective religious beliefs in his presence. Jews were represented by Jacob Ibn Killis, aided by someone called Moses. The Christians were represented by the 62nd Patriach of the Coptic Church, Pope Abram Ibn Zaraa the Syrian. His assistant was Anba Sawirus ibn Al-Muqaffa, the bishop of Ashmunin in Upper Egypt.

When the Jewish team seemed to be losing the debate, they appealed to the Caliph. They charged the Christians with hypocrisy, claiming they did not believe their own Scripture. They demanded that if Christianity was the true way, then Christians should be able to pray in terms of Matthew 17:20 and move mountains.

The Caliph agreed.

To the east of the city lay a rocky mountain. It would be convenient to have it moved. So, the Caliph gave Pope Abram a choice:

> 1) Prove the truth of Matthew 17:20 by praying for the mountain to be moved. If unsuccessful…

2) Accept Islam and abandon Christianity because its Scripture was false. Or…

3) Leave Egypt. Or…

4) All Christians to be killed by the sword.

Pope Abram asked for three days to consider the options, after which he would deliver his response. When this was granted, the Pope declared three days of prayer and fasting for all Christians in Egypt while he met with clergy.

The decision was to accept option one and to invite Simon the Tanner to pray on behalf of all. Simon was known for his ascetic lifestyle, piety and good works. Once when he was attending a customer who had come to have her shoes repaired, Simon noticed her leg. Lust entered his thoughts. In keeping with Matthew 5:28–30, he used his awl to remove one of his eyes.[48]

Simon agreed to be the one who prayed on condition that no one be told it was he who was doing the praying. He also instructed that after celebrating holy communion, at the appointed time the people were to pray "Kyrie Eleison" (Lord have mercy) one hundred times while facing each direction— north, south, east and west. Finally, the Pope was to make the sign of the cross over the mountain three times as clergy worshipped standing and sitting in silence while Simon, unnoticed, prayed.

Then it happened.

On the appointed day, estimated to be November 27, 979, as the worshippers stood, that which seemed like an earthquake swept the mountain lifting it up so sunlight could be see underneath it. When the worshippers sat the mountain was lowered. Three times this occurred.[49] The Caliph and his

---

48   Manuscript held in Auba Antonios Monastery, Egypt.
49   Inis El-Masri, *The Story of the Coptic Church.* Part 3, 27.

party panicked and begged the Pope to stop the worship, which he did.

Simon the Tanner could not be found. The mountain, now divided into three parts was named "Mokattam" (Arabic = *cut up*). The Caliph abdicated in favor of his son and entered a monastery. Although his leaving Islam is disputed by Muslim historians, for obvious reasons, a special baptismal facility appropriate for the immersion of an adult male was constructed in Saint Mecurius Church. It was named Maanoudiat Al-Sultun (Baptistry of the Sultan).[50] It is still there today.

Continued Blessing

After Egypt lost the 1967 war with Israel, Christians were blamed for the defeat. In 1969 the governor of Cairo ordered all Christian rubbish collectors to leave the city to live where they had been dumping the rubbish adjacent to Mount Mokattam. (The lowliest undesirable jobs are often reserved for Christians in Muslim jurisdictions.) On April 13, 1974, a church was started on the rubbish dump. Nine people attended.[51]

A few years later, the Coptic priest in charge, granted permission for a cave entrance to be cleared of rubble still there from "the earthquake" centuries ago. The emptied cave resulted in a giant open-air auditorium that seats 17,000 people. It is packed with people each week for a mid-week prayer and Bible study meeting. Prayer for healing continues till the early hours of the morning. Along one wall is a large warehouse. It is full of crutches, wheelchairs and similar paraphernalia left behind by those who no longer have need of them after being healed during the meetings.

---

50   Samuel Tadras, *Motherland Lost, The Egyptian and Coptic Quest for Modernity.* Stanford, CA, Hoover press, 2013, Vol. 638, 43, 53.

51   *The Biography of Saint Samaan the Shoemaker "The Tanner".* Cairo, The Church of Saint Samaan the Tanner, 1998, 83.

Local believers say this happens because the Lord has blessed the work through the prayers of Saint Simon the Tanner, who dared to step out in faith and claim Matthew 17:20. As Jesus said, "Everything is possible for the person who believes" (Mark 9:23).

We need to ask ourselves, "Does my faith move mountains or do mountains move my faith?" Real faith enables us either to remove mountains or to tunnel through. Faith sees the invisible, believes the incredible and receives the impossible. It helps us to walk fearlessly, run confidently and live victoriously. It enables us to go further than we can see (Hebrews 11:1).

> **Faith sees the invisible, believes the incredible and receives the impossible.**

We will know we are on the right path within the will of God, if having taken the first step, we have peace.

6. Peace

Through the prophet Isaiah God promised that for those who maintain faith in Him, He would keep them in perfect peace, because their minds were steadfast and trusting in Him (Isaiah 26:3).

The Apostle Paul made the same point. "...the mind controlled by the Spirit is life and peace" (Romans 8:6).

So, peace is a state of mind gifted by God. Jesus contrasted it with what the world calls peace. "Peace I leave with you, My peace I give you. I do not give you as the world gives" (John 14:27).

The world will never find peace for as long as it excludes God from its conference tables. The peace of which Jesus speaks comes when we adjust our wills to be in perfect harmony with

God's will for us. It comes after we have done God's will, not before.

It's difficult to describe because it is beyond our understanding (Philippians 4:6-7). But we know when we've got it, as surely as we know when we've lost it. If we have lost it we need to return to the last place where we knew we had it. After all there is no point in venturing further if we are heading in the wrong direction. A Jewish proverb reminds us that it is better to ask the way ten times than to take the wrong road once.

In all this process or journey we need to remember that we have a constantly present helper and guide, the Holy Spirit.

7. The Holy Spirit

As we pray, it sometimes seems that God is silent. For whatever reason we might have difficulty in hearing His response to our petitions. This causes us to imagine that we are abandoned to stumble when stepping into an uncertain future. At such times we need to remember that Jesus always delivers on His promises. He has given the Holy Spirit as a "Counselor to be with us forever", living with and in us (John 14:16-17). He teaches us all we need to know (John 14:25-26). He guides us into all truth (John 16:13). Assurance, knowledge and certainty that He imparts, is convincingly satisfying, beyond reasoned proof.

> God wants to bring us beyond the point where we need signs to discern His guiding hand. Satan cannot counterfeit the peace of God or the love of God dwelling in us. When Christ's abiding presence becomes our guide, then guidance becomes an almost unconscious response to the gentle moving of the Holy Spirit within us.[52]

---

52   Bob Mumford, Edythe Draper, editor, *Quotations for the Christian World*. Wheaton, Illinois, Tyndale House, 1992, 291.

When He nudges, He expects us to respond. Only as we take that first step does the next and the next become clearer.

A Chinese brother was trying to arrange delivery of a Christian book consignment. He had 15,000 copies and discreet storage was an increasing problem. As he was travelling, he had stepped into a railway office for a few minutes.

A pastor 2,000 kilometers distant was desperately searching for copies of the same book for his people. He knew who had them but had no idea where or how to find him. However, prompted by the Holy Spirit he dialed a random phone number. The phone rang in a railway office and was answered by the book distributor who was in that place for just 20 minutes.

The book of Acts is replete with examples of people and the church praying and waiting upon God for answers conveyed to them by the Holy Spirit.

Dr. Luke "... wrote about all that Jesus began to do and to teach" in the Gospel of Luke (Acts 1:11). In the Acts of the Apostles, he continues the story for 28 chapters. We are the subjects of Chapter 29 if we remain obedient and patient.

8. Patience

Ancient cultures learned something of which modern Western culture is almost totally ignorant—patience.

An old Greek proverb says, "One minute of patience gives ten years of peace."

Similarly, a Chinese saying is, "One moment of patience may prevent a disaster. One moment of impatience may ruin a life." But in our Western impatience, rather than wait for an egg to hatch we'd prefer to smash it open. If we were all farmers we'd want to plough in the morning, sow at midday and reap in the afternoon.

As Christians it's as if we pray, "God, grant me patience and give it to me right now."

The Bible, also reflecting an ancient cultural context reminds us that, "With the Lord a day is like a thousand years and a thousand years are like a day. The Lord is not slow in keeping his promise as some understand slowness" (2 Peter 3:8-9).

In other words, He operates on a spectrum totally beyond our restrictions and measurements of time. He is seldom in the same hurry as our busy little minds demand of Him. Our problem is that our culture has conditioned us to expect instant gratification as a right. So, we have instant soup, instant dessert, instant coffee, and instant wealth through gambling. Our wrist watches measure time in hundredths of a second, even though we will never use that measurement.

Our computers that enable us to communicate around the world in seconds need upgrading every couple of years as faster chips are developed and inserted. Supersonic propulsion has enabled us to position satellites that orbit the world in a few hours. But hypersonic will get us there faster. So that will become the preferred mode in the immediate future.

Our homes are filled with the latest consumer goods that cost much more than their ticket price, because we had to have them now and couldn't possibly wait until we'd saved the money to buy them. So, we flash our mobile phone or watch and click up another item on our already overloaded credit cards, the interest on which will be about 20% and compounding.

> **It is God who makes the promises. Faith believes it and hope anticipates it.**

When it comes to waiting on God for an answer to our

urgently placed prayer, should there not be an almost instant answer, we conclude that God has perhaps taken a holiday or has lost interest in us. So, we walk out on the relationship with Him to do our own thing.

We forget that the Bible says, "… Do not throw away your confidence. It will be richly rewarded. You need to persevere so that when you have done the will of God, you will receive what He has promised" (Hebrews 10:35-36).

Note, it is God who makes the promises. From a human perspective, faith believes it and hope anticipates it.

In our short fuse faith, we forget that it took 100 years for Noah to build his boat. God is not required to settle His accounts by the end of our financial year. We forget that God's promise to Sarah and Abraham was not fulfilled till they were respectively 90 and 100 years of age. We forget how long it took the angel to reach Daniel with the answer to his prayer (Daniel 10:12-13).

In my own experience as a cross-cultural worker, it took 12 years before we saw the first baptized believer from a previously unresponsive religious community. It took 25 years to fulfill God's direction to found a different sort of church in my home nation and to see it grow to one of the largest in the country. It took 30 years of experience and research for me to write *Mosques and Miracles*, which won the national prize for the best Christian book of the year.

Saint Vincent de Paul (1581-1622) was correct in concluding that "all comes at the proper time to him who knows how to wait."

When it is planted, Chinese bamboo seems to do nothing for four years. In the fifth year it suddenly shoots up 30 meters in 60 days. That is not the result of 60 days. It took five years to arrive at the precise conditions to achieve that result.

When rain falls on mountain slopes streams gush down to the plains below. As they surge, they seem to gurgle and sing as they swish around rocks in their path. If the rocks were removed all that would be left would be a muddy sluice which eventually would result in a destructive landfall occurring. Rocks and other obstacles are there for a beneficial purpose. Even so are obstacles and restrictions in our own lives. They are there not just to frustrate us, but to change us as we wait upon God.

By the time Georg Müller died, through the life of prayer and dependence upon God that he had lived, he was a vastly different person from what he was in his youth. His life became a powerful witness influencing many. Toward the end of his life, commenting on prayer, he said that the great point was never to give up till the answer came. Expressed in other words, we might say that after we have prayed, we need to hold on, hold fast and hold out.

Müller prayed for 63 years and eight months for the conversion of an acquaintance. He then commented, "He's not saved yet, but he will be. How can it be otherwise? I am praying." Shortly afterwards Müller died.

But as this acquaintance stood by Müller's open grave considering the impact his friend had and what God had achieved through him, it caused him to re-examine his own life. He softened, repented and determined that he also would follow the One to whom Müller submitted as Lord.

In the darkness of night, a plane attempts to land or a ship comes into port. In both cases, the pilot has different colored lights on the port and starboard sides. Only when they are all perfectly aligned, does the pilot know he is going to arrive safely.

Following all the principles outlined in this chapter will ensure a safer arrival on your journey toward fulfilling your destiny as you pray.

Chapter 5
HEARING HINDRANCES

Lord, what we know not, teach us.
What we have not, give us.
What we are not, make us.

St. Augustine (354–430)

Towards the end of the 7th century BC, the kingdoms around the Eastern Mediterranean region were shuddering. Babylon was the emerging superpower, having successfully challenged the fading Assyrian empire to become supreme. What remained of ancient Israel was in danger of annihilation. Unless God intervened, there was no hope.

Into that scene there stepped a prophet–Habakkuk. He complained to God about conditions within Judah. The rich were getting richer, while the poor were getting poorer. Homelessness was increasing. A breakdown of law and order was threatening. Justice was corrupted. The old order of respect for, and observance of, God's commands was passing away. Habakkuk railed against God's apparent inaction (Habakkuk 1:1–4).

God answered Habakkuk's complaint (Habakkuk 1:5–11), but Habakkuk appeared unable to hear it. The prophet continued his tirade about the circumstances as he understood them. He chided God for His seeming inactivity and His failure to respond to his complaints (Habakkuk 1:12–17).

In so doing, Habakkuk joined a tradition of other notables, Job (Job 21:7-9) and Jeremiah (Jeremiah 12:1; 14:9). They also could not comprehend the ways of the Almighty. To their embarrassment, they were later to learn that God had been fully aware of their situation. He was active. It was just another case of their failure to see what He was doing, to hear what He was saying, to understand that His ways are not our ways (Isaiah 55:8).

Still today, many of us are like those who have gone before, and find ourselves cast down into a pit of our own making. We believe in God. We believe the Bible. We attend church regularly. We affirm the Holy Spirit is ever available to guide us. But when the chips are down, when times get tough, when we desperately need reassurance that God is present and available to help us, for whatever reason we can't connect with Him. We call out and He seems so silent.

Like Habakkuk, in our rising frustration we become annoyed, irritable and even angry at God. Unless there is some resolution to the demands of our enquiry, we may give up, walk away and say God doesn't care. Bereft of faith in God, we may even join the growing numbers of atheists who, although they don't realize it, exercise an even greater faith. Despite all the evidence of history, science, creation, the existence of the Bible and the church, they choose to believe there is no God. Often this happens because we didn't get what we wanted when we wanted it. So, we resort to the crutch of agnosticism or atheism, to support us as we limp hopelessly toward eternity.

The other option is to stay the course and to ask questions, even of ourselves. Could the fault, our inability to hear, be not with God, but with us?

Evelyn Christenson was a pastor's wife. She met with two prayer partners weekly to pray for their church. However, as weeks ticked by, they sensed they were not making any headway. It was as if God had turned a deaf ear to their petitions. It seemed odd, but they felt that their attention was being directed to a particular verse in the Bible.

"If I had cherished sin in my heart the Lord would not have listened" (Psalm 66:18).

At first, the thought that this could apply to them seemed ridiculous. They were good, morally upright, church-attending ladies. They were hardly to be equated with drug dealers, bank robbers, fraudsters or any of that parade of malefactors who regularly occupy the headline space of sensationalist media.

But as they more honestly opened themselves to be exposed to whatever the Spirit might reveal, they were dismayed to learn that within them there were issues of pride, self-satisfaction and critical attitudes all neatly covered with pretense.[53] Isaiah's word would hit home hard.

"Your iniquities have separated you from God.

Your sins have hidden His face from you so that He will not hear" (Isaiah 59:2).

So many of us cry out to God while continuing to cherish unconfessed sin. It is that very sin that separates us from Him.

There are references in the Bible that speak of unconfessed sin resulting in God's relationship with His people being severed. We need to be aware of this and, whenever the need arises, examine our own lives to see where the problem lies.

In God's sight there are neither big nor small sins— just sin.

53   Evelyn Christenson, *What Happens When Women Pray.* Wheaton, Illinois, Victor Books, 1975, 23-25.

In God's sight there are neither big nor small sins—just sin. Should we be aware of any in our own lives, how society might rank them is unimportant. Whatever there is needs to be confessed and forgiveness asked for, as preliminary steps to restoring our relationship with God (1 John 1:9). The reward will be that we then may be able to hear more clearly what He is saying to us.

Let's look at a few of the common sins which we tend to overlook or disregard.

1. Unforgiveness/Criticism

These two are commonly inseparable twins. Jesus warned: "If you do not forgive men their sins, your Father will not forgive your sins" (Matthew 6:14-15).

He added: "If you hold anything against anyone, forgive him so that your Father in heaven may forgive your sins" (Mark 11:25).

So important did Jesus regard the danger of unforgiveness and its presence in our lives, with its capacity to inhibit our relationship with God He added: "If you are offering your gift at the altar and there remember that your brother has something against you, leave your gift there in front of the altar. First go and be reconciled to your brother; then come and offer your gift" (Matthew 5:23-24).

If we do not forgive, then the danger is that not only is our relationship with God threatened, but we also will suffer with a "root of bitterness" (Hebrews 12:14-15) growing within that will poison so many other relationships.

If there is any unresolved issue between us and another, regardless of whose fault we may consider it to be, unless we act to get it sorted out, we may pray all we like, but those prayers will hardly ascend beyond the ceiling, let alone reach heavenly realms.

For anyone who considers themself an aggrieved party, forgiveness seldom comes easily. But Jesus regarded it as being so fundamental to spiritual health, He didn't just commend it, nor did He just ask us to forgive. He commanded us to do it. And in the very words of Jesus, obedience to His teaching and commands, is the acid test of the ultimate proof of our love for Him (John 14:15, 23). This obedience results in the Father's love for us and in Jesus revealing Himself to us (John 14:21).

John Hyde was a missionary in India. One day as he prayed, he felt a burden to pray for a certain national pastor. In his prayer he rehearsed the unfortunate mannerisms and seeming coldness of the pastor. But then it seemed as if a divine finger touched Hyde's lips. He believed he heard God say to him, "He who touches that pastor touches the apple of my eye."

Hyde immediately exclaimed, "Father, forgive me. I have been an accomplice of Satan. I have been an accuser of the brethren before you."

Hyde realized that the easiest thing to find was fault in others. But those who throw mud never have clean hands. So instead of being negative and critical of the pastor, Hyde asked God to show him good things in the pastor's life. As these came to mind, Hyde praised God for this man.

Shortly thereafter revival broke out in the pastor's church. A blockage preventing that happening sooner was Hyde importing his critical attitude into his prayer life.[54]

An 89-year-old quite unwell Christian lady had been in and out of hospital so many times, that she just wished to die to go to be with Jesus. "Why doesn't He hear my prayer?" she asked. For weeks she seemed suspended between time and eternity. When she was again in hospital, one of her sons while visiting her, suggested a new thought to her. Perhaps the Lord

---

54   Dick Eastman, *No Easy Road*. Grand Rapids, Michigan, Baker Book House, 1971, 33.

was keeping her here because of some unfinished business. But what could it be?

Gently the son raised a matter that had caused his mother great distress for years. Decades previously her husband had divorced her, after she had given years of exemplary service as a wife. She had brought up four sons almost unaided, because her husband was often absent for months looking for work. She had worked hard on their small farm. When her husband was seriously injured in an automobile accident and was permanently disabled, she ceaselessly cared for him. But as he was about to receive a significant sum of money as an insurance payout for the accident, which could have provided financial security for the first time in their long marriage, he divorced her! Humanly speaking she had every reason to feel hurt and even angry.

Although many years had gone by since the divorce, nevertheless the son raised the issue, "Mother, perhaps the unfinished business for you relates to whether you have ever forgiven your husband and our father. If you haven't perhaps this is why your prayer is not being granted."

With tears in her eyes, she admitted she had never forgiven her husband. But as they talked of how Jesus had forgiven her and her husband, who just before his death became a believer, her heart softened. Together mother and son prayed. She had forgiven at last. Very shortly thereafter, she departed on her glorious journey into eternity with Jesus.

In some societies such as those in the West, daily news is dominated by protest marchers demanding their "rights", by parliamentarians hurling their abuse at their opponents, by communities claiming victim status, by media that sells by headlining negativity. It's so easy for Christians also to flow with the harsh, critical, unforgiving, entitlement-oriented spirit of our age. That needs to be resisted.

Even without the teaching of Jesus, we should be inspired to go countercultural by the life and witness of Nelson Mandela of South Africa. He saved his nation being torn apart in leading by example, forgiving those who had imprisoned him unjustly for 27 years and then establishing the Truth and Reconciliation Commission.

> For the development of one's spiritual capacities, a full diary leads to an empty heart.

A Turkish soldier had beaten a Christian prisoner until he was only half-conscious. As he continued to kick him, he shouted, "What can your Christ do for you now?"

The prisoner replied, "He can give me the strength to forgive you."[55]

2. Indiscipline

The noblest of all forms of government is self-government, but it is also the most difficult. Personal indiscipline may often be a hindrance to hearing what God is saying to us.

A dividing line between success and failure may be expressed in five words—"I did not make time." The reason we don't make time is because in practice we don't rate the matter as being sufficiently important, even though we might say otherwise.

When Paul challenged Roman Governor Felix to respond to the claims of Christ, Felix replied, "That's enough for now. When I find it convenient, I will send for you" (Acts 24:25). It was a brush-off. He never did send for Paul. In his mind, the matter just wasn't important enough.

---

55   R. Earl Allen, *Quotable*. Ministries Today, July/August 1997, 16.

If something is considered of lesser importance, we procrastinate doing anything about it. We can never catch up with good intentions. Lost time is never found. We allow the urgent to replace the important. For the development of one's spiritual capacities, a full diary leads to an empty heart.

We can spend much time working for the Kingdom of God but fail to spend time with the King himself. The substitute for blessedness is often busyness, which leads to barrenness. We become too busy to love, too busy to share or care, too busy to pray. We need to discipline ourselves to set God honoring priorities.

God says, "Be still and know that I am God" (Psalm 46:10).

Former British journalist, Malcolm Muggeridge (1903–1990), once said, "God is the friend of silence, because He speaks only when we are quiet."

After an operation for cancer and just prior to his death, English evangelist David Watson wrote, "God showed me that all my preaching, writing and other ministry was absolutely nothing compared to my love relationship with Him. In fact, sheer business had squeezed out the close intimacy I had known with Him."[56]

Sister Briege McKenna, a lady to whom God gave a powerful healing ministry, made a commitment to spend three hours a day with God in prayer. She said:

> I've had to remind myself continually that I need Jesus more than people need me. If I don't go to Jesus in prayer, I would have nothing to offer them. I don't pray because I am holy, but because I want to become holy and I need Jesus to teach me. We forget sometimes that Jesus is a living person who waits for us. When we pray, we are not committing time to a project but to a living person. Jesus

56   Jim Graham, *Prayer*. London, Scripture Union, 1985, 23.

is there not for what I can give Him but for what He gives to me.[57]

Charles Mahaney told of how for years he struggled to become consistent in prayer. Finally, when he asked the Lord why he was unable to pray more, he got an unusual response. He said, "I wasn't ready for the answer the Lord gave. Expecting an insight that I had yet to hear in all my study of the subject, the reply came, 'You're lazy!'"[58]

Mahaney had trouble getting up in the morning because he was undisciplined in going to bed sufficiently early. He had to realize that God did little in his life after 10:30pm.

The Apostle Peter wrote that we need to be, "clear minded and self-controlled so that (we) can pray" (1 Peter 4:7). He further added that self-control leads to perseverance and perseverance leads to godliness (2 Peter 1:6). Without self-control, perseverance and discipline, we will never set and keep to priorities needed to develop a relationship with God that He desires for us.

Idolatry is the third area worth checking.

3. Idolatry

Several centuries before Jesus' time on earth, Israel's leader, Samuel, challenged his nation, "If you are returning to the Lord, then rid yourselves of the foreign gods and the Ashtoreths and commit yourselves to the Lord and serve Him only, and He will deliver you" (1 Samuel 7:3).

There was good precedent for the demands Samuel was making. Centuries earlier Jacob had done likewise. Under God's instruction Jacob and all the members of his household were setting out on a journey. They were to proceed to Bethel, the name of which means *House* or *Place of God* (Genesis 35).

---

57   Briege McKenna, *Miracles Do Happen*. London, Pan Books, 1987.
58   Charles Mahaney, *Why don't I pray more?* Pastoral Renewal, April 1986, 145-147.

This was the place at which Jacob had first encountered God as he was fleeing from the wrath of his brother, Esau (Genesis 28).

However, he well knew that, with the passing of the decades since that first life changing encounter, typically of all humans, other things had crept into their lives to displace the preeminent place that belongs to God. He knew that the one requirement for a meeting with God was holiness. If he and his family were to meet with and hear from the Almighty, they had to prepare adequately for that. So, he said to all in his household:

> "Get rid of the foreign gods you have with you, and purify yourselves and change your clothes. Then come, let us go up to Bethel where I will build an altar to God who answered me in the day of my distress and who has been with me wherever I have gone" (Genesis 35:2-3).

The temptation to replace God with someone or something else in our affections is ever present and will remain till the end of our days. According to the Bible, even after a third of humankind will have been killed by plagues and other disasters warning of divine retribution for our rebelliousness, the remaining two thirds,

> "... still did not repent of the work of their hands; they still did not stop worshipping demons and idols of gold, silver, bronze, stone and wood, idols that cannot see or hear or walk. Nor did they repent of their murders, their magic arts, their sexual immorality or their thefts" (Revelation 9:20-21).

Contemporary history bears witness to the fact that we are well on the way to fulfilling the specifics of Revelation outcomes. Of course, in supposedly "Christian" cultures we may no longer carve in wood, metal or stone images, before which we worship or to which we direct prayer. That activity may be left to the renaissance of witchcraft in our midst in this 21st century. But in more subtle ways, many more of us may be guilty of slipping gently into this sin.

William Ullathorne (1806-1889) succinctly summed up the situation as follows:

> "Whatever a man seeks, honors or exalts more than God is idolatry."

If that is so, how else may we define the effort expended by many, to climb the greasy pole of professional promotion? To obtain status aren't we willing to clamber over the backs of others? What are we to make of the desire to have titles before our names and letters after them? How else do we explain our ambitions to live in excessive McMansion houses, upgraded regularly and to have the best home and garden in the street? Equally questionable is our frequent trading in of our multiple automobiles or having our children attend only the best schools. Our desire for instant gratification that leads to permanent indebtedness, sees us seeking to assuage our chosen credit agencies more than God Himself, as we entrap ourselves in endless debt by our desires to obtain whatever we want—now!

In our over commitment to surround ourselves with the trinkets of modern lifestyles, we demonstrate our real priorities, among which there is often little room for Him whom we say is Lord in our lives. If that is the case, prophecy delivered through Ezekiel may apply, "These (people) set up idols in their hearts and put wicked stumbling blocks before their faces. Should I let them enquire of me at all?" (Ezekiel 14:3).

Achan sold himself for expensive cloth and a wedge of wealth (Joshua 7:20-22). Ahab traded his life for a vineyard (1 Kings 21). Judas bartered his life away for a bag of coins (Matthew 26:14-15). Each of their lives ended in disaster.

If we allow anything to occupy that preeminent place in our lives that belongs exclusively to God, then this becomes our form of idolatry. For some of us that might include family ties, our denominational certitudes, or even personally inspiring religious leaders, whom we promote to infallible celebrity status. Our deceitful hearts {Jeremiah 17:24} are ever capable of repurposing whatever God may have provided and through the assembly line of our inventive thoughts, reproduce convenient self-satisfying idols.

If that is so, we should not be surprised if God's response to us is the same as it was in Ezekiel's day. Twenty-five leaders of the nation who appeared so upright and righteous on the outside, had each set up secret idols for themselves. They mistakenly thought that the Lord would not notice their activity. But He did. His response was swift and severe. "… I will deal with them in anger; I will not look on them with pity or spare them. Although they shout in my ears, I will not listen to them" (Ezekiel 8:12–18).

4. Disobedience

If our communication with the Lord is disrupted, an obvious question to ask concerns the possibility of disobedience in any area of our lives. From the beginning of humankind's creation, intimacy with God was dependent upon the sole condition of obedience (Genesis 2:16–17). Our difficulties today in communion with our Creator, are directly attributable to our forebears' disobedience (Genesis 3).

But because of what Jesus has done on our behalf, communication is restored (Romans 5:19). However, it remains so, based upon the

God doesn't want

our success.

He wants us.

same condition at creation–obedience. Jesus said, "If you remain in Me and My words remain in you, ask whatever you wish and it will be given you" (John 15:7).

Decades later the Apostle John confirmed the same principle. "We receive from (God) anything we ask because we obey His commands and do what pleases Him" (1 John 3:22-23).

God doesn't want our success. He wants us. He's not grading us in terms of worldly achievement. He's requiring our obedience. Obedience is the key that admits entry into every spiritual vault, or procession into the innermost sanctuary of God's presence. What we think, know or believe is almost irrelevant, compared to whether we are obedient. Even Jesus had to learn that (Hebrews 5:8). The opposite outcome is achieved by disobedience. "God's wrath comes on those who are disobedient" (Ephesians 5:6).

Obviously, if we are in a state of attracting God's wrath, then we should accept that open communication with Him will not be restored, until we repent and demonstrate that by both word and deed. "If I had cherished sin in my heart the Lord would not have listened" (Psalm 66:18).

5. Wrong Motives

The Bible says: "When you ask, you do not receive, because you ask with wrong motives…" (James 4:3). It also says: "If we ask anything according to God's will He hears us" (1 John 5:14).

So, the question arises, when we pray, what is our real underlying motive? If we are attuned to God's will, we have every reason to be heard and to receive appropriate answers? But if not…?

Unfortunately, because of our inbuilt tendency to put self first, even our seemingly altruistic prayers on behalf of others, may be little more than a cloak of deception over our real motives. For example, we may pray for fine weather to enable farmers to gather in their crops. But our real motive is to provide sunshine for our beach holiday.

We may pray earnestly for the salvation of a member of the opposite sex. But this may be only a means of concealing our own romantic interest in that person. "The heart is deceitful above all things and beyond cure. Who can understand it?" (Jeremiah 17:9).

Even our most sacred task, communion with our Heavenly Father, may be polluted by our own deceitfulness and our reluctance to examine our true motives. It is easy to pray in terms of our self-fulfillment, that we may build our own kingdom rather than God's Kingdom. We prefer to have our desires satisfied rather than be brutally honest with our motives in prayer.

A businessman prayed long and hard about how much he was desirous and willing to contribute financially to God's work through the local church. Yet when God did not grant accelerated prosperity to his business, that man walked away from God and his association with the local church. Clearly, his motive in praying was not that he might be a means of prospering the work of the Kingdom of God. It was more about increasing his personal prosperity. Years later he admitted, "God didn't grant my prayer, so I walked away."

God does not deal with us based on any self-centered motives. It's only as we align with the attitude of Jesus—"Not My will but Your will be done" (Mark 14:36)—that we should expect open communication with our Maker.

A woman who attended a prayer seminar testified as follows:

> My initial reaction to the prayer seminar was what good will it do? I have prayed and prayed and it hasn't done any good. I have been a Christian all my life. Now my

husband's construction company has folded, leaving enormous debts. We have had to sell our home, liquidate our assets and also our young son has just undergone surgery.

For some time, I have been praying for what I wanted to happen. Suddenly I saw something new. I had not prayed for God's will to be done. So, I said aloud, "Lord, I want Your perfect will for me and my family."

That was it. I was to learn what was keeping my prayers from being answered was that I had never asked God for His will. Now I am free. The whole load is lifted. The responsibility to straighten out this mess is no longer mine and at last I know peace. My husband's debts are being paid. My health has improved. I was offered a job when I wasn't searching for one. This new train of events started once I totally surrendered my will in every matter to the will of God.[59]

"Not my will Father, but Yours be done" is often the opening for which God waits before He is able to speak into our lives in terms we can understand.

6. Doubt

Doubt is a normal part of the human condition. If someone is told there are 63 billion stars in the universe, they'll usually believe it. But if they encounter a sign that says, "Wet paint," they mostly won't believe until they have touched the paint themselves. In this they are no different from the Apostle Thomas. Despite all the testimony to the contrary, he doubted Jesus could have come back to life, until Jesus Himself invited Thomas to touch Him (John 20:27).

Thomas stood in a long Biblical tradition of doubters. It started with the serpent planting seeds of doubt about God's

---

59   Christenson, 55-56.

goodness in Eve's mind. Doubt has been the devil's dog ever since.

Despite all the miraculous signs and wonders God had done in delivering the Israelites from bondage in Egypt, when it came time to enter the Promised Land they doubted (Numbers 13).

When Elijah was emotionally empty, he doubted God would continue to protect and enable him, so he prayed to die (1 Kings 19:4).

John the Baptist was regarded by Jesus as the greatest man who had ever lived (Matthew 11:11). Yet in prison he doubted that Jesus was really the long-awaited Messiah (Matthew 11:2-3).

In the spiritual realm doubt tells us there may be no God or, if there is, He doesn't care about our situation. Such a mindset literally has deadly results.

According to a study published in the *Archives of Internal Medicine*, doubt can hasten death among sick patients. In 1996, 596 hospital patients surveyed were wondering whether God had abandoned them or still loved them, because of the illness they were enduring. Compared with others who had a more positive outlook, it was demonstrated that this cohort was more likely to be dead within two years.[60]

Doubt sees the obstacles; faith sees the way.

We know that the antidote to doubt is faith. Doubt makes mountains that only faith can remove. One anonymous writer summed up the relationship between the two as follows:

---

60   Marshall and Susan Shelley, *When the soul cries out.* Moody, March/April 2002, 11.

Doubt sees the obstacles; faith sees the way.
Doubt sees the darkest night; faith sees the day.
Doubt dreads to take a step, faith soars on high.
Doubt questions, "Who believes?" Faith answers, "I".

In the normal events of daily life, doubt may be faith under construction. But if such attitudes are permitted to infect our prayer life, the result is a foregone conclusion.

"When (anyone prays they) must believe and not doubt, because (the one) who doubts is like a wave of the sea, blown and tossed about by the wind. That one should not think he will receive anything from the Lord; he is a double minded man, unstable in all he does" (James 1:6-8).

To the doubter God seems silent. The problem is not with God but with the doubter's inability to hear anything from God, because of the ramblings of his own skepticism and doubt. Closely linked to doubt, there is another hearing hindrance which is widespread among Western Christians—unbelief. John Drummond (1851-1897) defined the difference between the two thus:

Doubt can't believe; unbelief is won't believe.
Doubt is honesty; unbelief is obstinacy.
Doubt is looking for light; unbelief is content with darkness.

7. Unbelief

In a village about 70 kilometers distant from Hefei, the capital of Anhui province in China, two women established a church. The cost of a church building was 20,000 Yuan. Because the Sunday offerings were only 20 Yuan, it was fortunate that the husband of one of the women was a building contractor. He supplied most of the materials and labor. When construction was complete, they were obliged to register it with the

Government's approved Three-Self movement. It was either register or have the building destroyed.

When it came to evangelism and church growth, unlike in the West, the ladies literally followed our Lord's example.

From conversations with doctors at the local hospital, they learned which cases were beyond medical help. For these terminal patients they would then begin to pray. Should they discern that it was God's will that any should live and not die, they intensely prayed accordingly.

In one 12-month period they saw 20 such cases in which people were healed of "incurable" diseases—mostly cancer. Through this ministry the numbers in the church increased from zero to 200.

In one particularly challenging case, as the ladies prayed fervently, the family of the ill person threatened violence and ordered them to desist. But they persisted. After 20 days the person was healed. Uneducated, barely literate but with a passionate love for the Lord and people, they were used of God to establish His church against opposition and the threats of persecution.[61]

When was there last a similar story of a church planting process in the West? The church that God has built over the last 70 years in China may be the greatest ever seen in human history. It has thrived despite relentless persecution, unmatched except in the earliest centuries of church history.

The church in the West depends upon its affluence, theological institutions, well-educated clergy, world best technology and the precision of its doctrinal statements. And it is dying. China has little of those resources. Theirs is a simple childlike faith. They pray persistently. They love Jesus passionately. They accept the

---

61   Compass Direct editors, *China: the daft, the daring and the dark.* Momentum, September/October 2005, 41.

Bible unquestionably. These are today's true believers.

In the West we say we believe, but live lives of practical atheists. We so order our affairs as to never have to put God to the test. Our ingrained attitudes lead to widespread spiritual power failures. With our carefully camouflaged unbelief in prayer, we retreat into vague generalities. According to the measure of our faith, we ask God for little outside of our own control. And that's exactly what we receive—little or nothing.

God doesn't expect the impossible from us. He wants us to expect the impossible from Him.

Prayer becomes like window-shopping as we flit from subject to subject. As with window-shopping, it's an enjoyable way to pass the time. It costs nothing. It results in nothing. We do this because we doubt God's ability to deliver on His amazing promises.

When we come to God, we need to remember that we are not just coming to the all-powerful, all-knowing King of Kings. We are approaching our Heavenly Father. He is vitally concerned about the minutest detail of our daily lives.

The Apostle Mark records the story of the man with a demon-possessed son who no one else was able to help (Mark 9:14–32). Driven by compassion and desperation demanded by the situation, he implored Jesus, "If You can do anything, take pity on us." To which Jesus replied, "If I can? Everything is possible for him who believes."

The distressed parent groaned, "I do believe. Help me overcome my unbelief." If we would hear God, the confession of a pained parent is as good a place to start as any.

American evangelist D.L. Moody is quoted as saying, "God doesn't expect the impossible from us. He wants us to expect the impossible from Him."

Chapter 6
PRAYER—UNANSWERED?

*It is when God appears to have abandoned us
that we must abandon ourselves most wholly to God.*

François Fénelon (1651–1715)

The woman, a journalist, still trembled when she retold what had happened.

> Late on a black noiseless night in upstate New York, I decided to take a shortcut home up a steep, unlit path. Then I heard footsteps behind me, faster than my own. An instant later the man was upon me, tightening my new striped scarf around my neck, while ripping at my pants.

> At home her mother woke from a deep sleep, seized with fear that something terrible was about to happen to her eldest daughter. The mother immediately knelt beside her bed and prayed. For 15 minutes she begged God to protect her daughter from the nameless real threat she felt her daughter faced. Convinced she had won God's attention—and protection—the mother returned to bed and a sound sleep.

> Back on the stony path the would-be rapist suddenly ceased his assault. He cocked his head, almost beastlike and fled down the hill.[62]

A remarkable answer to prayer?

---

62   Kenneth L. Woodward, *Is God Listening?* Newsweek, April 1, 1997, 61–62.

There are many even more amazing answers to prayer recorded in the Bible. One of them is found in 1 Kings 18. The prophet Elijah was on top of Mount Carmel. Before him on an altar lay two bulls readied for sacrifice. All morning the 450 priests of Baal had chanted, danced and begged their god to let fire fall from heaven and thus prove he was greater than Jehovah. The heavens seemed singularly unimpressed. Nothing happened.

Then Elijah stepped forth. He ordered that the whole altar and the wood around it be soaked with water—not once, but thrice. When everything was drenched, he called out to God to demonstrate that He alone was the true God, by sending fire from on high to incinerate the sacrifices on the altar. Immediately fire fell burning up the animals, wood, stones, water and even the surrounding soil. As a result:

> "When all the people saw this, they fell prostrate and cried, 'The Lord, He is God! The Lord, He is God'" (1 Kings 18:39).

How exciting it is to find God dramatically answering prayer instantly. It's equally exciting when something similar happens today as in the case of the journalist. Such interventions are not confined to nominal Christian domains.

A Muslim convert to Christianity received a phone call as he worked in a government office in South Asia. The caller advised him that fire had broken out near his home. It looked as if nothing could save his simple dwelling. He rushed home and had time to remove a few of his possessions as flames threatened to engulf his house. Unable to do anything else the man stood still, raised his hands and voice toward heaven and called out asking God to save his home. Muslim neighbors who had been hostile toward him for leaving Islam, watched to see what might happen. As the new believer finished his brief and desperate prayer, there was a clap of thunder. Torrents of rain poured down and extinguished the fire.

His erstwhile persecutors were impressed by his seemingly new relationship with the God of the Bible. Allah of the Koran never answered the supplications of his devotees in such a way, despite their five times a day entreaty.

So, whether in the East or the West, God dramatically intervenes to save His children in answer to their urgent pleas for help. True. But for whatever reason often things turn out differently.

In the same country in which the new believer's house was saved from fire, another new believer experienced a different outcome. He also was a convert from Islam to Christianity. According to the various schools of established Sharia Law, for adult males of sound mind, if they leave Islam and refuse to return, the penalty is death. For women it is imprisonment.

This new follower of Jesus was caught by his neighbors. They demanded he leave the infidels and return to the ummah, the worldwide community of Muslims. He refused. So according to established practice, to persuade him of the error of his ways, to relieve his family and village of shame and to restore honor, they proceeded to cut off his fingers. Still, he would not recant. So, they cut off his hands, tied him to a tree and left him overnight to reconsider his position. When they returned the next morning, he was dead.

However, in the meantime news of what was happening had reached media outlets in the capital city. By the time reporters arrived to investigate and write up their versions of what had happened, the corpse had been hung from the branch of a tree. The media investigators were told that the poor fellow was so ashamed of his flirtation with apostasy, that he had committed suicide by hanging himself.

This outcome begs the question, what happened here? Did this man and some of his new friends not pray? If they did, did God turn a deaf ear and choose not to respond? Doesn't the Bible say, "Call to Me and I will answer you and show you great and mighty things which you do not know" (Jeremiah 33:3)?

Didn't Jesus say, "Whatever things you ask when you pray, believe that you receive them and you will have them" (Mark 11:24)?

Didn't Jesus further say, "If two or three of you agree on earth concerning anything that they ask it will be done for them by My Father in heaven" (Matthew 18:19)?

Didn't the Apostle John record Jesus as saying, "The Father will give you anything you ask in My name" (John 16:23)?

Because there are so many seemingly broad, sweeping, almost unlimited precious promises studded throughout the Scriptures, can we not as some suggest, simply "name it and claim it"?

If that is so, why is it that we also read, see, hear and experience ourselves, with a degree of frustrating frequency, that God does not seem to answer our prayer? And in this regard, we are in excellent company.

One of the finest men, the noblest of fellows who ever walked the earth, was a person called Job. He was upright in character, with a well-deserved excellent reputation. Yet in the blink of an eyelid, he went from prosperity to penury, from riches to rags, from good health to humiliating illness.

The greatest king Israel ever had was David. He is recorded in history as being, "...a man after God's own heart" (Acts 13:22). If anyone had a good relationship with the Almighty, it was King David. But when his baby was ill, although David lay prostrate on the ground fasting, praying and begging God to save the child's life—the boy died (2 Samuel 12).

The Apostle Paul was early Christianity's greatest missionary church planter and theologian. Thirteen of his written works are included in the New Testament. His ministry was characterized by words, works and wonders (2 Corinthians 12:12). Again, if anyone had a good relationship with his Creator and an excellent understanding of God's ways, it was this man, Paul. Yet when he prayed to be relieved from a troubling affliction, nothing happened. The only answer he got was, "My grace is sufficient for you, for My power is made perfect in weakness" (2 Corinthians 12:9). Seemingly God considered that it was better for Paul to remain humbled than healed, that he be dependent rather than independent.

In any gathering of believers there may be found so many who have prayed for a job but still haven't found one. Prayer unanswered? There are often parents who have prayed for their children who in turn decide to go their own way leaving behind a trail of grief and disappointment. Prayer unanswered?

Frequently students pray fervently for help with exams only to learn when the results are published that they have failed. Prayer unanswered? Many watch their loved one's struggle with pain and disease while they plead with God for healing. But the loved one died. Prayer unanswered?

In most congregations there are numbers of singles who have begged God for a spouse, yet none has arrived. Prayer unanswered? There are so many children who have prayed for their parents, yet separation and divorce were the bitterly contested outcome. Prayer unanswered?

There are others who for years have prayed for their spouses and other close relatives that they might find Jesus, submit and become citizens of the Kingdom of God. But they have seen no change. Prayer unanswered?

> **God is not a celestial banker with whom we can lodge withdrawals from our credit account.**

When war breaks out, many believers pray for a return to peace. But the war continues leaving many people distraught, damaged or dead. Prayer unanswered?

How do we respond to these kinds of situations? Will we pretend they don't exist, try to deny or ignore them?

Often in the stunned silence of disappointment, ceaseless questions reverberate around the empty chambers of our numbed minds. "Why? What have I left undone? Was my faith inadequate? How else could I have prayed? Why this? Why now? Is there no answer?"

Only very gradually do we come to understand that God is not a celestial banker with whom we can lodge withdrawals from our credit account. Nor is He a heavenly vending machine into which we can lodge a token and receive an instant reward.

So how do we cope?

From ancient times others have posed similar questions.

"Why, O Lord, do You stand far off?
Why do You hide Yourself in times of trouble" (Psalm 10:1)?
"Why do You hold back Your right hand?
…Why don't You destroy my enemies" (Psalm 74:11)?
"Does He who implanted the ear not hear" (Psalm 94:9)?
"How long, O Lord must I call for help, but You do not listen" (Habakkuk 1:2)?
"…You cannot tolerate wrong.
Why then do You tolerate the treacherous?
Why are You silent" (Habakkuk 2:13)?

Recently as our evening meal was being cooked in our electric oven, suddenly the power to the oven switched off. We didn't think that because there was now no power being delivered to the oven, that the electric company as a long trusted and effective source of energy, no longer cared for us. Neither did we think that power was only available to favorites or to those who believed the right things about electricity. We immediately set about finding exactly what had caused the power failure, so that we could fix it and have power restored as before.

The same principle should apply when we discover our prayer power connection to God has been severed. From what we know of God, the fault will not be with Him. The Bible identifies at least 25 probable causes for this happening and every one of them has to do with us. To explore all of them would deliver a volume that few could afford to buy or give time to read. So, let's look at the most common causes.

Common Causes

1. Sin

This is the commonest cause for seemingly unanswered prayer.

The Israelites had been explicitly ordered by God to "turn around and set out toward the desert along the route to the Red Sea" (Deuteronomy 1:40). But in a fit of arrogance and rebellion they decided instead to enter the Promised Land to challenge the Amorites in battle. They were smashed. As Moses later said, "You came back and wept before the Lord, but He paid no attention to your weeping and turned a deaf ear to you" (Deuteronomy 1:45).

Years later when the commander-in-chief of Israel's army, Joshua, pleaded with God for a military victory after their crushing defeat at Ai, it was denied. (Joshua 7) In the toughest

> ## Access to the ear of God is not the common right of humanity.

way possible God needed to teach the people that they must be obedient to His commands. If not, they would end up as little more than a nameless band of ill-disciplined, plundering marauders. They would ultimately be lost in the dustbowl of history like many others who rose and fell, who came and went.

Sin—disobedience to God's dictates—was in their midst. It had to be exposed, rooted out and dealt with. Until that happened, they could expect only continued disaster.

As previously mentioned, King David begged God to save his son whose mother was Bathsheba. God did not grant his pleadings. The boy died. David had sinned. He knew it. But rather than face the consequences of his adultery, he made matters worse. He had tried to use prayer as a crutch to cover his own sinfulness. God would have none of it (2 Samuel 12:16-22). Through bitter experience he learned a lesson.

Much later he could say:

"If I had cherished sin in my heart, the Lord would not have listened" (Psalm 66:18).

Still later the prophet Isaiah would expand the principle:

"Surely the arm of the Lord is not too short to save, nor His ear too dull to hear. But your iniquities have separated you from your God; your sins have hidden His face from you, so that He will not hear" (Isaiah 59:1-2).

Access to the ear of God is not the common right of humanity. It is a privilege extended by the King of Kings. Those who scorn His Lordship, flout His laws and spurn His grace, can hardly expect to have Him to do their bidding when they call.[63]

2. Selfishness

A more subtle yet equally common cause for unanswered prayer is selfishness.

From personal experience the Apostle Paul could testify with certainty that irrespective of circumstances, "My God will supply all your needs" (Philippians 4:19).

However, there is a significant difference between wants, wishes and genuine needs.

Another Apostle, James, expressed it thus: "When you ask you do not receive because you ask with wrong motives that you may spend what you get on your pleasures" (James 4:3).

Simply invoking the name of Jesus in a prayer does not automatically oblige God to answer. The question is what motives are unstated behind our prayer?

We might pray, asking God to bring judgment on sin and sinners because we know that God hates sin. But our personal motive may be the hope that God will wreak vengeance upon those we don't like. All the while in so praying we focus upon our perception of sin in others' lives while avoiding closer inspection of our own lives.

We pray for Kings, Princes, Presidents, and Prime Ministers, because we are enjoined to do so for civil authorities (1 Timothy 2:1-2). But often our real motive is to see the fulfillment of our own preferred political party's triumph over all others.

This was on view for all to see in the 2020 Presidential elections in the USA. Millions on the conservative side of politics, aligned with and prayed for the reelection of President Trump.

---

63   Lynn Cox, *Prayers God Cannot Answer*. On Being, August 1992, 10.

Many self-appointed prophets prophesied President Trump's reelection. When that didn't happen, only a few courageously admitted their mistakes and resigned from their self-appointed office of "prophet". Many others continued to claim that their prophecies were true and, declaring that the election was stolen, said Trump was still the real President.

Having attempted to recruit God to fulfill their own political agendas, they compounded their mistake when they lacked the moral fortitude to admit their error. Prayers motivated by self-interest are always dangerous. They might just be granted—with even more disastrous aftereffects.

2 Kings 19 tells the story of how the kingdom of Judah, in the reign of King Hezekiah, was miraculously rescued from destruction by the invading Assyrian forces of Sennacherib. At that time, Hezekiah was affected by a terminal illness (2 Kings 20). Instead of accepting God's will as best for all, Hezekiah begged for a reprieve of lengthened life. Amazingly he was granted an additional 15 years.

Instead of being humbly grateful for this extension, Hezekiah became rash, foolish and vain. He flaunted the nation's wealth to a foreign delegation. His action sparked Babylonian greed. Hezekiah was next advised that these foreigners would one day carry off all the royal wealth and his very own descendants would be transported into exile and abused as slaves. Hezekiah was unperturbed. All he cared about was his own welfare. Things went from bad to worse.

Hezekiah fathered a child during this time with a wife, Hephzibah. Her name is omitted from the list of kings' mothers in 2 Chronicles. Therefore, according to the established custom, it may be concluded that she probably was not of Israelite birth. This was another error of consequences on Hezekiah's part. At age 12, the son Manasseh, became king on his father's death.

He married Meshullemeth from Jotbah in the Sinai Peninsula (2 Kings 21:19). She also may not have been an Israelite woman.

Thereafter followed a descent into pagan depravity, till Manasseh after 55 years on the throne "was buried in his palace garden…of Uzza" (2 Kings 21:18). Uzza was the name of an Arabian astral god. Here was another indication of how far the nation had sunk in breaking its covenant with Jehovah.

The future was sealed. The nation had brought upon itself its own destruction. The woeful chain of events resulted because one man, King Hezekiah, would not accept God's best. Focused upon his own self-preservation, he prayed a feverously selfish prayer, the outcome of which was the destruction of his own nation.

Beware of selfish prayer.

3. Meanness

Nothing reveals our true spiritual state as accurately as how we handle our money. A Latin proverb says money is always our master or our slave. The Apostle Paul considered the love of money as being "the root of all kinds of evil" (1 Timothy 6:10). Others have claimed it is the parent of all wickedness. Jesus considered the subject of such importance, that about a fifth of all His teaching was about money.

As money may represent such a potential for evil in our lives, John Wesley (1703–1791) found a possible solution to neutralize its allure. He reportedly said, "When I have any money, I get rid of it as quickly as possible, lest it find a way to my heart." He lived according to his own teaching. Through his voluminous writings and other income streams, it has been calculated that in the equivalent of today's values, millions of dollars flowed through his hands. Before he died, he reportedly said, "If I leave behind me ten pounds, you and all mankind bear witness against me that I lived and died a thief and a robber." Upon his death it was learned that his estate contained sufficient to cover the costs of his funeral and some silver cutlery that he used at mealtimes.

The Bible says we are to "honor the Lord with (our) wealth… then (our) barns will be filled to overflowing and (our) vats will brim over with new wine (Proverbs 3:9–10). Elsewhere it exhorts us to "give and it will be given to you" (Luke 6:38). Many have proved the truth of these principles by implementing their advice.

However, others overlook the consequence of not following these instructions. The Bible carries an implicit warning when it adds, "For the measure you use it will be measured to you" (Luke 6:38). The implication is that unless we give according to our income, God may reduce our income according to our giving.

Most believers know that "it is more blessed to give than to receive" (Acts 20:35). The problem is that many are far too willing to let the other person experience the blessing. Rather than give according to their means, they give according to their meanness. When confronted with the needs of others, the only time they put their hands in their pockets is during cold weather. They never learn that the open hand holds more friends than the closed fist.

As we pray, we are promised, "we receive from (the Lord) anything we ask" (1 John 3:22). But that assurance is found within the context of generously contributing towards the needs of others.

Even more alarmingly we are warned, "If a person shuts their ears to the cry of the poor, they too will cry out and not be answered" (Proverbs 21:13).

If prayers are going unanswered, it's good to check out one's attitudes towards money and the record of our own generosity, toward the needs of others.

4. Relationships

A fourth reason for seemingly unanswered prayer is the state of our relationships with others. None is more sensitive or sacrosanct than that of marriage. Some say that marriages are made in heaven. Others, noting that not all marriages end happily ever after, would argue that according to the Bible there's no marrying in heaven. That's why it's heaven.

Regardless of where one lands on the sentimentality scale on judging the God-ordained institution of marriage between a man and a woman, one thing at least is certain. After the eager sprint to the altar to exchange rings and vows, what follows is akin to a marathon. Having hopefully *found* the right person, each must ever after live to *be* the right person. Marriage is not a gift. It is more an achievement. Its foundation is God. By the actions of each, the edifice is slowly constructed day by day.

However, as national statistics of divorce show, being a practicing Christian no longer ensures success. Whenever something ruptures the harmony between married couples, their spiritual lives are affected. The Apostle Peter, speaking to husbands, told them to be "… considerate toward (their) wives and (to) treat them with respect as heirs of the gracious gift of life, so that nothing will hinder (their) prayers" (1 Peter 3:7).

If the sacred relationship of Biblical marriage is impaired to the point where it becomes less than God-honoring, then our relationship with our Heavenly Father is also affected. Our prayer life will be "hindered."

Husbands and wives may be active in Christian service. Externally they may present as the perfect couple. But if that is inconsistent with what is happening domestically, removed from view from outsiders, then it is a sham. God is not fooled. There will be an urgent need to restore intimacy with each other before intimacy with God should be expected.

5. Timing

A fifth reason for seemingly unanswered prayer is timing.

The writer of Hebrews said: "Do not throw away your confidence; it will be richly rewarded. You need to persevere so that when you have done the will of God, you will receive what He has promised" (Hebrews 10:35-36).

Norvel Hayes proved the truth of those words. When his marriage broke up, as a single dad he did the best he could in trying to care for Zona, his teenage daughter. Things went well until Zona decided to marry her boyfriend, Bobby. As Norvel prayed, he believed God had shown that they should not marry at that time, but to wait. Zona refused to listen. Her friends told her that Norvel was only a doting controlling father. Ignore him. So, Zona and Bobby married. One year later they were divorced.

Angry and rebellious, Zona found her own lodgings and drifted deep into drugs and debt. As Norvel kept praying, Satan repeatedly discouraged him by reminding him he had been a failure as a father.

After praying for 6 months, Norvel began to wonder if God was listening to his prayers. With more time and still no change in Zona's behavior, Norvel's doubts only increased. God didn't seem to care. After two years and still no change in circumstances, Norvel was convinced. God wasn't listening any more to his daily prayers.

But then he had a visitation from the Holy Spirit who encouraged him to "stand in the gap," to keep praying for his daughter with unswerving faith. He was also to tell Zona how much he loved her.

In praying, Norvel became more aggressive, declaring that Satan could not steal his daughter away because she was coming back to the family of God. Then Zona and Bobby remarried. Norvel considered this to be a repeated disaster. Still, he continued to pray for another year.

Then, one evening the young couple turned up at a conference where Norvel was speaking. At the end of the meeting, they came to the front of the auditorium seeking prayer. With that, the Holy Spirit fell on them so strongly that Bobby fell to the floor.

After years of praying, Norvel's prayers were answered because:

- At the beginning he acknowledged his helplessness.
- He trusted God to do what he could not.
- While hating the sins he loved the sinners and told them so.
- Daily with unswerving faith and trust, with relentless tenacity, he prayed on.[64]

There are various reasons God may delay answering our prayers. The process of causing maturity is one. The Apostle James knew about this.

> "Consider it pure joy, my brothers, whenever you face trials of many kinds because you know that the testing of your faith develops perseverance. Perseverance must finish its work so that you may be mature and complete not lacking in anything" (James 1:2-4).

The maturation process cannot be accelerated.

When the promise of a child was given to Abram and Sarai (Genesis 15), 25 years passed before that promise was fulfilled.

---

64   Leonard Le Sourd, *Stand in the Gap for Your Children*. The Intercessors, Vol.4 No. 8, Breakthrough Inc., Lincoln, VA, December 1984.

The timing of that delay was to highlight the fact that the birth of Isaac was no natural event. It was a supernatural process superintended by God Himself.

When Mary and Martha appealed to Jesus to come quickly because His friend Lazarus was dying, he deliberately delayed (John 11:1-44). By the time He finally arrived, Lazarus was dead and buried. Was Jesus being callously uncaring? Far from it. His delay was to exemplify dramatically a much greater truth than His power to heal illness. By raising the corpse of Lazarus from death, it demonstrated that Jesus had power not only over sickness but over our greatest enemy—death itself.

Luke 11:1-13 records what we call "The Lord's Prayer". It might be referred to more accurately as "The Disciples' Prayer". It was given to them as a model in response to their request to be taught how to pray. This prayer is followed immediately by an unforgettable story illustrating that in prayer, we are not to give up but to persist till the answer comes (See Luke 11:5-13).

For many of us, having prayed a little about various matters, having not received any answer, we consider that we have somehow failed. That presumption of failure becomes the path of least persistence. During difficult times, we cease trying when with persistence we might well have achieved the breakthrough we seek.

In cross-cultural ministry among a very resistant people in South Asia, because of lack of response for over a century, new staff arriving in the 1960s also did not know what to do. Slowly as they prayed and as God redirected them into different ways, results came. It only took 12 years for the first fruits to be harvested. But because of what they and others were doing, a national magazine, a further 14 years on, claimed that "preliminary statistics are really amazing as the number of converts are reaching almost 100,000."[65] A different

---

65   'Faith Tragedy in Bangladesh', Al-muslimoon Weekly, January 9 1994.

national investigation concluded, "It is spreading very fast and contagiously like AIDS virus and destroying Islam."[66]

Persistence in prayer pays.

A sixth reason for seemingly unanswered prayer, is very common but is the most difficult to understand.

6. The Best

When we are buffeted by the turbulence of trouble or assaulted by doubts and difficulties, we are comforted by the assurance, "that in all things God works for the good of those who love Him, who have been called according to His purpose" (Romans 8:28).

> God is always actively at work in our lives to effect what is in our own best long-term interest.

To emphasize the point, the Apostle Paul later added that, "God is working in us to will and to do His good pleasure" (Philippians 2:13).

Therefore, we can assume that God is always actively at work in our lives to effect what is in our own best long-term interest. In this He is more concerned with our holiness than our happiness. The ways He chooses to achieve His objectives may not meet our limited self-centered expectations. But in the end the outcome proves to be the best.

When Peter, James and John were on the Mount of Transfiguration, they suddenly saw Elijah and Moses conversing with Jesus (Matthew 17:1-13). Thinking that this was as good as it could ever get, they wanted to erect a shelter that would probably develop into a shrine. Their plan was to stay there.

---

66 Religious Survey-7, 90-96AD Narsingdi Zone-9, Islamic Missionary Council of Bangladesh.2.

Had Jesus agreed, the three of them would never have become Apostles to the world. A far more glorious calling awaited them than being caretakers of a shrine.

Later when Jesus was praying at Gethsemane, aware of what lay ahead, torture, assumption of the sin of the whole world, death, separation from the Father, He asked if it wasn't possible to avoid this (Matthew 26:39). As events showed the request was denied. Had it been granted, there would not have been any death on the cross, any shed blood, any atonement, any forgiveness of sin, any defeat of death and no hope for humanity. Of course, Jesus willingly accepted the Father's determination on the matter. The outcome was infinitely the best for fallen humanity.

Zachariah and Elizabeth, descendants of Aaron, were a blameless, upright, righteous, godly couple (Luke 1:5-6). For years they had prayed for a child. It never happened. Elizabeth remained barren. In society's eyes their marriage was a failure. They were shamed. Personally, their dreams were unfulfilled. They could have assumed their prayer was denied or that God was not interested in them.

But after years of waiting, an angel arrived and told Zachariah that their prayers had been heard and were granted. Because both were now in advanced years, Zachariah couldn't believe it. But in the Lord's perfect timing a son was born. They named him John. He was hugely distinguished in God's sight (Luke 1:15). He would influence the nation and the world (Luke 1:17). He was to announce the arrival of Jesus. Jesus in turn said that John was the greatest person who had ever lived (Matthew 11:11).

From the point of view of John's parents, the delayed answer to their prayers was insufferable. From God's perspective the timing was precisely impeccable. The outcome was unimaginably the best.

A lump of iron or steel isn't worth much. If it is beaten into horseshoes, its value increases slightly. If made into needles its value is further enhanced. If that same lump of metal ends up being turned into springs for watches, its value is multiplied beyond comparison with what it was in its original state. Even so does our value increase as we are used to fulfill God's purposes. By this process we are subjected to refining fires of adversity and beaten into shape through prolonged times of waiting upon God for His answers to our prayer.

Pastor Rick Warren and his Saddleback congregation commenced their new work. In so doing, they could never have imagined that it would take 13 years of delays and failed attempts before they were able to find God's choice of 113 acres for the land for their church. It was 15 years before they erected the first building. In the meantime, the congregation had grown to 10,000 people without a home base. This was unprecedented in American church history. But through the journey, God fashioned a pastor and a people of such integrity, that they have influenced their nation and beyond. As Pastor Rick testified, "Delays are not necessarily denials. God's ways are better than ours—and His timing is perfect."[67]

In 1994 during the 50th commemoration of D-Day, the anniversary of the landing of allied troops on the shores of France in the Second World War, two interviews were recorded. One was of a soldier who, on that day in 1944, had waded ashore and engaged in the battle at ground zero. He concluded that from his perspective, "I was convinced that there was no way that we could possibly win the battle."

The second interviewee was a pilot who on the day had been flying high overhead. He said, "From my perspective I was convinced that there was no way that we could possibly lose the battle."

---

67   Rick Warren, *Encouraging pastors and church leaders with tools for healthy, growing churches.* Pastors.com, Issue 224, September 14, 2005 (Viewed January 28, 2006).

> **When God seems silent faith rests content.**

Similarly, God always has a better perspective from His vantage point than we do from ours. "As the heavens are higher than the earth, so are My ways higher than your ways and My thoughts higher than your thoughts" (Isaiah 55:9).

The issue is not whether we get what we want when we want it, but whether we will continue to trust in God, to believe that He is good, kind, generous and wanting that which is best for us. Faith is not defined by answers God gives in response to our prayers. Rather it is our response when He seems not to answer at all.

When God seems silent faith rests content.

Even should His answer be "no", we are to remain grateful that He cares sufficiently to deny the immediate for the sake of something better in our future. In our childish mindset, we need to remember that often we are too immature to see what lies ahead.[68]

The response of some people who experienced adversity was that they cursed God (Revelation 16:21). The contrary response was that of Job. He lost all his possessions, his children and then was afflicted with illness and pain. So extreme was his misfortune that his wife suggested that he, "Curse God and die!" (Job 2:9).

Throughout this testing time Job's response was: "Naked I came from my mother's womb and naked I will depart. The Lord gave and the Lord has taken away; may the name of the Lord be praised" (Job 1:21).

---

68   R. Wilkinson, *Unanswered Prayer—A Trial of Faith*. New Life, March 11, 1993.

Appropriately, the commentary on Job's response was: "… Job did not sin by charging God with wrongdoing" (Job 1:22).

Periods of seemingly unanswered prayer confront our impatience with a choice. We can curse God and walk away. Or we can embrace them as growth opportunities. In that case, stumbling blocks of doubt become steppingstones toward deepened faith and intimacy with God.

The example of the Psalmist is worth noting:

"Will the Lord reject forever?
Will He never show His favor again?
Has His unfailing love vanished forever?
Has His promise failed for all time?
Has God forgotten to be merciful?
Has His anger withheld compassion?" (Psalm 77:7-9).

Having confronted these age-old questions, he gives an answer: "I will remember the deeds of the Lord. Yes, I will remember Your miracles of long ago" (Psalm 77:11). "… as for me, I will always have hope: I will praise (the Lord) more and more" (Psalm 71:14).

As preachers have often said:
When the conditions are not right, God says, "No."
When the time is not right, God says, "Slow."
When you are not right, God answers, "Grow."
When everything is right, God says, "Go."

Chapter 7
LEAST USED MOST NEEDED POWER SOURCE

An intercessor is one who is in such vital contact with God and with his fellowmen that he is like a live wire closing the gap between the saving power of God and sinful men who have been cut off from that power.

Hannah Hurnard (1905–1990)

Arthur Blessitt, an American evangelist well-known in the latter half of the twentieth century, knew what it was to pick up his cross and follow Jesus. He did that literally, through endless trekking over decades walking through more than 100 countries. The cross he carried had two small wheels attached to the base of the upright, while the crosspiece lay over his shoulder. In a video of his travels called, *Arthur, A Pilgrim*, he recounted some of his adventures. One of these that brought him close to death was in Nicaragua in 1979.

It was early morning when seven gunmen burst into the camper trailer where he was sleeping. They lined him up outside and readied to shoot him. However, his one thought was that he wasn't going to die without his Bible. So, he dived back into the trailer to get one.

Instead of his own Bible, he picked up a carton full of them thinking he would give one to each of his killers before they shot him. But when he returned, none of the gunmen remained standing. Six were on the ground about five meters away and one lay half in half and out of the trailer door. Blessitt approached each of his attackers offering water and a Bible. All refused. With a look of terror on their faces they fled.

Later he learned that at the time of the threat, back in the United States, friends had been awoken with the urge to pray for his safety. One of them prayed that God would send 12 big angels to fight for him right at that time. When other friends, who had been inside the trailer emerged, upon surveying the scene, they asked Blessitt if he had hit the men. He hadn't but obviously someone had.[69]

In the Bible

Examples of prayer offered on behalf of others are sprinkled throughout the Bible. In Exodus, Moses interceded on behalf of the whole nation (Exodus 34:8-9). Later Samuel did likewise (1 Samuel 7:5). Later still it was David pleading with God for mercy on behalf of his people (1 Chronicles 21:16-17). Isaiah prophetically foretold that one of the ministries of Jesus would be intercession (Isaiah 53:12).

That's precisely what we see Him doing during His earthly ministry. So, He prayed for Peter (Luke 22:32) and for the future church (John 17:9). He even prayed for His enemies as He was being tortured to death on the cross (Luke 23:34). And now He sits "at the right hand of God and is interceding for us" (Romans 8:34). This is His forever ministry (Hebrews 7:25). It is the longest continuous prayer meeting in history.

The Apostle Paul also asked for intercessory support (Ephesians 6:18-20).

Oswald Chambers (1874-1917) summed up the process thus: Jesus carries on intercession for us in heaven; the Holy

---

69   Arthur Blessitt, *Arthur, A Pilgrim*. Video 1978.

Spirit carries on intercession in us on earth; and we the saints must carry on intercession for all people.

George Sweeting, a former Chancellor and President of Moody Bible Institute, noted that: Church history demonstrates that the decades of spiritual power were also decades of great praying. Yet despite this knowledge, our generation suffers a dearth of prayer.[70]

> Church history demonstrates that the decades of spiritual power were also decades of great praying.

This is not a new phenomenon. In the days of Isaiah, when his nation had gone astray, "The Lord looked and was displeased... He was appalled that there was no one to intercede" (Isaiah 59:15–16).

Still No One?

Almost three millennia later we still have learned little. As the first chapter in this book makes amply evident, there is a very high correlation between prayer and what happens in the church and nation. Admittedly correlation is not causation. But the linkage is so obvious, it can never be discarded or ignored. However, while we don't completely discard it, in practice we mostly seem to ignore it.

Some decades ago, I submitted my doctoral dissertation to the examining authorities of what was the largest fully accredited interdenominational institution in the world at that time. I was advised that in all their years of operation, prior to my submission, they had never received any dissertation related to the subject of prayer and church growth!

70   George Sweeting, *Wanted Intercessors*. Moody, May 1993, 62.

As long ago as 1986, research done by church growth and missions' scholar, Dr Win Arn (1932-2006), reported that 80 to 85 percent of American churches were either plateaued or in decline.[71] Pastors, avoiding the embarrassing absence of fruitfulness, consoled themselves by emphasizing faithfulness.[72]

The situation is much more serious today. In the United States Progressive/Liberal denominations are in free fall. Decline is also happening in Conservative denominations. The largest of them, the Southern Baptists, recently announced in an annual report that, in that year, they baptized only the same number of people as they did decades previously in 1948. The same trend is far more advanced in other Western countries.

Media presence of mega-churches conveys the false impression that all is well. But without exception, in every Western nation, the percentage of practicing Christians is in serious continual decline, while non-Christian religions such as Islam, Hinduism and Buddhism are growing rapidly in their midst. They are filling a spiritual vacuum created by Christianity vacating the scene.

Former aerospace engineer, John Beckett, noticed what was happening in his nation. He saw:

- Society plunging headlong toward secularism.
- Moral restraints being removed.
- Progressively liberal education.
- Devastating decisions by the court system.
- Dependence on science and technology in attempting to solve all human problems.
- Loss of cutting edge within churches.
- Neglect of proclamation of the Gospel and adherence to its demands.

---

71   Win Arn, *Growth Report*, Number 13, 1986.
72   Daniel Griffiths, *God's Awesome Few*. Ministries Today, November/December 1988, 38.

He decided to act. He resigned his job, set up his own organization and founded an intercessors movement.[73]

In the Old Testament, the role of intercessor seems to focus upon individuals praying on behalf of the nation. Hence the Lord's disappointment when He couldn't find even one person to "stand before (Him) in the gap on behalf of the land" (Ezekiel 22:30).

In the New Testament, the emphasis would appear to shift from the individual to the corporate, specifically the church. Jesus, the Lord of the Church, "always lives to make intercession for (us)" (Hebrews 7:25). But in that all believers "are a chosen people, a royal priesthood, a holy nation, a people belonging to God" (1 Peter 2:9), we are meant to join with Jesus, to exercise our priestly function interceding on behalf of others. By "others" is meant individuals whose needs are known to us, various types of leaders in Church and State, nations or the whole world.

Leading With Prayer

Movements and organizations that are led by people of prayer, are certain to make a difference between floundering or flourishing. When the China Inland Mission (CIM/OMF) was searching for the successor to its founder, Hudson Taylor, they chose D.E. Hoste (1861-1946). He led the mission from 1900 to 1935. Colleagues at that time commenting on the appointment of Hoste said,

> ...(they) needed a man who could give time to prayer and thus get to know the mind of the Lord... It was his prayer life that impressed those who knew him more than anything else. Intercession for his fellow missionaries was

---

73   John Beckett, *Are You an Intercessor?* Restore, November 1985, 23-26.

regarded as his first duty toward them and was put before everything else.[74]

When a multi-cell organization such as the church, in all its varied forms and congregations, takes seriously its responsibility to intercede for its nation, the outcome can be dramatic. Churches in South Korea normally start each day with a prayer meeting at 5:00am. Those prayer meetings in which everybody prays aloud simultaneously, sound like rolling thunder. They pray against the spiritual powers and principalities that they believe affect life in their nation. The evidential outcome can't be ignored. While in most Western countries the church declined throughout the twentieth century, in South Korea it grew from almost zero to forty percent of the nation. Despite two wars that devastated the country, they have been blessed with world-leading industry, education and affluence.

The Korean church prays not just for the nation, they pray for leaders and pastors. Christian leaders are especially in need of intercession. In ministry, the further pastors go in effectiveness, influence and visibility, the more they will be targeted by Satan and his many willing helpers.

A Southern Baptist leader reported the following:

> During a recent flight I took from Detroit to Boston, I sat next to a man who kept bowing his head as though he was praying. I asked him if he was a Christian. He looked shocked at my question. "Oh no, you have me all wrong. I am not a Christian. I'm a Satanist."
>
> I asked him what he was praying for as a Satanist. He looked at me stonily. "My primary attention is directed

74   Phyllis Thomson, *D.E.Hoste "A Prince with God"*. London, CIM, Lutterworth Press, 1947, 95.

toward the fall of Christian pastors and their families living in New England."[75]

When a leader falls, many others are likely to be taken down and out as well. There is an ever-growing list of international Christian leaders who have been obliged to resign from their ministries, in the late years of the twentieth century and on into the twenty-first. One wonders, did they not have any to whom they were transparently, honestly accountable? And even more importantly, had they not recruited intercessors to pray specifically, not just for their ministries but also for them personally?

Levels of Intercession for Leaders

Church Growth specialist, C. Peter Wagner (1932-2016), identified three levels of intercession:

- I-1. Intercessor-Level One. This person has a relatively intimate relationship with the leader. There is open two-way communication. This intercessor may be a relative, spouse, adult child or close, mature, long-standing, trusted friend. Seldom would there be more than three of these inner circle intercessors.

- I-2. Intercessor-Level Two. These are in regular contact with the leader, but the relationship is more casual. For example, commonly they could be church members who pray regularly for their pastor.

- I-3. Intercessor-Level Three. These have no regular contact. The relationship is more remote and depends upon correspondence, newsletters or digital correspondence.[76]

---

75   C. Peter Wagner, *The Least Used, Most Needed Power Source.* The Breakthrough Intercessor, Volume 10 Number 1, January/February 1990, 1.

76   C. Peter Wagner, *Intercession as Power—And as a Gift of the Spirit* (Part 2). Ministries Today, November/December 1987, 82.

Effects of Intercession

Recently I was battling five illnesses simultaneously in my body. For four of them at present there is no known cure. On a "down" day I received a text message from an I-2 intercessor. The message relayed that on the night before, this intercessor who didn't know much about my personal predicament, had a dream. The dream was about how many people were praying for me. Within five minutes, I received another text message from an I-3 intercessor who lives on another continent. He advised, wholly unbeknown to me, that had been praying daily for me for over 40 years! As these messages were coming in, an I-1 intercessor arrived sensing I needed extra prayer support immediately. I was encouraged!

Wagner recounted how one of his intercessors was responsible for saving his life. On March 25, 1983, he was on a ladder in his garage when he fell headfirst onto the concrete floor three meters below. At that time, an intercessor was 24 kilometers distant attending a school concert. Suddenly, she felt an overwhelming sense of evil, death and destruction come upon her. For 20 minutes she prayed against whatever was happening. The burden lifted. She later learned that this battle was exactly the time of Wagner's fall. Normally, an accident such as he sustained, would have been fatal. Subsequent X-rays showed that not even one of Wagner's bones was broken.[77]

So more precisely who is an intercessor? Yonggi Cho (1936–2021) defined an intercessor as, "a person who stands between God and an urgent need and pleads to God for that need."[78]

According to the prophet Ezekiel, God searches for such people (Ezekiel 22:30). Often their prayer and fasting will be

---

[77]   Wagner, *The Least Used Most Needed Power Source*. The Breakthrough Intercessor, Volume 10 Number 1, January/February 1990

[78]   David Yonggi Cho, *Answers to Your Questions*. Seoul, Church Growth International, 1984, 48.

accompanied by mourning as they identify with situations that also cause God grief (Joel 2:12).

These spiritual activists are not out on the streets waving placards and shouting slogans. They are found often alone, wrestling with prayers of petition, as they "bear not only their own burdens, but also the burdens of those for whom they are praying."[79]

They pray believing and "...expecting God's will shall be done in the here and now, on earth, as it has been established there and then, in the spiritual realm of the heavenlies through the cross and the resurrection!"[80]

This is not a ministry for new believers. But with a little mentoring, patience and practice, any believer may become an intercessor. It's like learning to play a piano. Master Chopsticks and scales first, before following a vision to become a concert soloist playing Chopin or Beethoven.

One of the most encouraging things one believer can do for another is summed up in just four words, "I'm praying for you." As a minister of the Gospel, I appreciate that any intercession by others on my behalf is always "powerful and effective" (James 5:16).

As I sign books written by me, I often include Ephesians 6:19, "Pray also for me that whenever I open my mouth, words may be given me so that I will fearlessly make known the mystery of the gospel, for which I am an ambassador in chains. Pray that I may declare it fearlessly, as I should."

For the many decades I have been in ministry, I would never have survived without the intercessors team I personally recruit and keep informed through monthly communication. Without these invaluable partners, I might not "finish the race

79   Eddie Smith, *Seven Habits of Praying People*. Ministries Today, March/April 1998, 45.
80   Jack Hayford, *The Church on the Way*. Grand Rapids, Chosen, 1983, 110–111.

and complete the task the Lord Jesus has given me—the task of testifying to the gospel of God's grace" (Acts 20:24).

Elsewhere, it was mentioned how reluctantly D.L. Moody went to preach in a church in London. It was a Congregational church in North London. Because the morning congregation seemed so unresponsive, Moody tried to get out of preaching the same night. But Pastor Lessey wouldn't hear of it. The response in the evening service to Moody's preaching was unprecedented. Later it was found that the difference in responsiveness between services, was because of a single intercessor praying ceaselessly throughout the day for Moody's evening meeting. But it didn't stop there.

Moody had moved on to Dublin. But he was recalled to London to handle the revival that had broken out. Hundreds of people were converted and added to churches across North London, through the brief series of meetings at which Moody preached. This led to an invitation for him to return to England, for a much greater harvest that had international implications.

In Moody's own church in Chicago, there was always a stream of conversions, not just on Sundays but almost on every day of the week. It continued when R.A. Torrey followed as Pastor after Moody's retirement. Torrey was followed by A.C. Dixon—and the phenomenon continued. Torrey attributed it to the men and women who

> "... sat up late Saturday night or rose early Sunday morning to pray for (the) pastor... It was not so much the men who were preaching as the people behind them who were praying that accomplished great things for God."[81]

To this Dixon testified:

> ".... any church can have a minister who is a man of power, a minister who is baptized and filled with the Holy Ghost,

---

81   R.A.Torrey, *The Power of Prayer*. Grand Rapids, Zondervan, 1987, 38-39.

if they are willing to pay the price, and the price is prayer, much prayer and much real prayer, prayer in the Holy Ghost."[82]

> **It's not only pastors who need intercessors. All Christians do.**

It's not only pastors who need intercessors. All Christians do. But missionaries often have a more urgent need, especially if they are embedded in less developed, or hostile environments.

Every two weeks a medical missionary serving in a hospital in Africa, rode his bicycle to a nearby city to collect supplies. It required him to camp out in the jungle overnight. On one of his visits to the city, he treated a local person who had been wounded in a fight. Several weeks later, the same man approached him in the city and told him how he and his friends had followed him into the jungle with the intention of killing and robbing him. But as they waited for the missionary to go to sleep, they noticed he was surrounded by 26 armed guards. The missionary dismissed the story as no more than a ludicrous flight of fancy. But the would-be assailant and his friends insisted they had fled, fearful of the guards.

As the missionary was later retelling about the event in a church in Michigan (USA), a man jumped to his feet and interrupted him with a question, "Can you tell me the exact date when this happened?" When the missionary advised the group of the date, his interrupter continued,

> "On that night in Africa it was morning here. I was preparing to play golf. As I put my bags in the car, I felt the Lord leading me to pray for you. In fact, the urging was so strong that I called the men of this church together

---

82   Torrey, 40.

to pray for you. Will all those men who met with me that day please stand."

The men who had met on that day to pray together stood—all 26 of them![83]

Elsewhere in Africa, a team of missionaries was travelling through a desert when a windstorm caused them to become disoriented and lost. Within two days their water supply was finished. Dehydration quickly followed. As they prayed, suddenly they came upon an unexpected pool of water. Their thirst was relieved. After marking the place, they continued their journey and found their way back to safety. Later when they returned to their life-saving pool there was nothing there. It no longer existed. Intercessory prayer had moved God to save them.[84]

Timely intercession can positively affect entire communities.

Transforming a Village

In April 1999, Christian families in Saltillo in Chiapas State, Mexico, were attacked and expelled from their homes because of their evangelical faith. Caciques—traditional community leaders—threatened to kill them if they returned. The government eventually allocated a piece of land for them to establish their own village, where they would also be free to follow their faith. The new village was called Annexo Saltillo Chacala. There was one problem—the land was completely barren. Repeated attempts to grow local crops resulted only in failure.

By the time other Christians discovered their plight, the local believers were destitute and starving. A team of intercessors decided to pray over the merciless land and ask God to

---

83   Tim Kopp, *The Case of the 26 Prayer Warriors*. London, African Evangelical Mission fax, January 23, 1997.

84   Paul Yonggi Cho, *Prayer is Intercession*. New Day, August 1991, 7.

bless it. Prayers were said in Dutch, Spanish, English and Tojalabal—a local dialect.

Five years later when the prayer team returned, they found the granite ground covered with grass and wild plants. Rain had fallen in abundance. Fruit trees,

> **Intercession is the strongest tool to break open the hardest places.**

flowerbeds, vegetable plots, domestic animals and chickens were everywhere. New houses were interspersed among hundreds of acres of flourishing maize fields. Now those who had driven them out were saying they wished someone had driven them out, because the land where the believers lived was more blessed than their former land ever was.[85]

Transforming a Nation

Nations can be changed through intercession. Colombia had the infamous distinction of being the cocaine center of the world. Criminality was endemic. Multiple homicides were a dangerous daily occurrence. Then the church in Cali started to organize citywide prayer meetings. For 11 years they persisted with their all-night prayer vigils.

On March 24, 2005, 50,000 people assembled to pray in the local stadium of Cali for the twenty-first time. They were joined by prayer vigils held simultaneously in 95 other cities, towns and villages throughout Colombia. In the following week reported homicides dropped by 60.9 percent.[86]

Intercession is the strongest tool to break open the hardest places.

---

85   *The Power of Prayer.* Open Doors, November 2005.
86   *Transformation Continues in Cali, Colombia.* http://archive.openheaven.com/forums/
      printer_friendly_posts.asp?TID=3701, April 22, 2005 (viewed April 23, 2005).

Transforming the World

In October 1993, 20 million people combined to pray for the 62 countries in which 97% of the world's least evangelized peoples live. In the next year, Christians in those target countries reported revival sweeping through their villages, unprecedented openness to the message of the Gospel and Jesus frequently appearing to believers in dreams and visions, to announce that He was the Son of God.

In Senegal, pastors publicly repented of their disunity and committed to future cooperation. Healings and supernatural manifestations followed.

In India, the number of enrollees in a Vacation Bible School doubled to one million children. Another mission agency reported a doubling of decisions made for Jesus through their literacy program.

In Tibet and Bhutan, previously totally closed countries, the first house churches were established. In Albania, the number of churches doubled.[87]

Intercession can save a nation from civil war.

In 1994, South Africa faced a very real possibility of civil war. The scene was bleak as the nation faced its imminent day of reckoning—national elections. Tensions, violence and social chaos increased as economic activity, peace and stability decreased. With the leaders of various tribal, racial and political interest groups at loggerheads, many anticipated a bloodbath. Apartheid and white supremacy looked like being replaced by riots, fighting and the splintering of South Africa into conflicted ethnic groups.

Then, Michael Cassidy, founder of *African Enterprise*, summoned Christians to a Jesus Peace Rally in Durban to be

---

87   *Prayer Campaign Results in Changed Nations.* Ministries Today, November/
       December 1994, 88.

held on April 17. By April 15 peace negotiations had broken down. Zulu tribal leader, Chief Margosthu Buthelezi, had left the deadlocked negotiations. Without him and the Inkatha Freedom Party he founded back in 1975, progress toward a political solution was impossible. He had already flown out for Ulundi. But then his plane suddenly developed problems and was forced to return to Lanseria airport. There Professor Washington Okumu, a Christian from Kenya, had just arrived to attempt to facilitate a reconciliation among the conflicted parties. While Okumu and Buthelezi spent more time in negotiations, 30,000 Christians in the local stadium were praying to God for a successful outcome, to keep the nation united without loss of life.

Finally, a deal was brokered that permitted Dani Schutte, the man in charge of the election process, to proceed toward that immediate goal. Over the next three days the elections were held. "They were the most peaceful days in the country's history."[88]

On April 19, the Chief Minister announced that God had saved South Africa from civil war. Secular newspapers are not noted for pious commentary. Yet four of them described what had happened as a "miracle". They also reported that the incidence of violence had plummeted and tensions had eased.

Nelson Mandela became President. An unprecedented spirit of reconciliation swept the nation. The new South Africa was born. The first verse of its National Anthem adopted in 1997, reflected the nation's dependence upon God who heard His intercessors and answered so dramatically.

> Lord, bless Africa.
> May her glory be lifted high.
> Hear our prayers.
> Lord, bless us Your children.

---

88   African Harvest, Summer 2022, 1–2.

So much for stadium-sized crowds and nation changing intercessory events. But how can an individual operate specifically and effectively when alone?

Intercessor's check list

Experienced New Zealand intercessor, Joy Dawson (1926-2022), offered widely reported advice on one way of going about intercession:

1. Make sure your heart is clean before God by having given the Holy Spirit time to convict, should there be any unconfessed sin (Psalm 66:18, 139:23-24).

2. Acknowledge you can't really pray without the direction and energy of the Holy Spirit (Romans 8:26).

3. Die to your own imaginations, desires and burdens for what you feel you should pray (Isaiah 55:8; Proverbs 3:5-6, 28:26).

4. Ask God to control you utterly by His Spirit and thank Him for doing so (Ephesians 5:18; Hebrews 11:6).

5. Praise Him for the remarkable prayer meeting you're going to have (2 Chronicles 16:9; Ephesians 1:9).

6. Deal aggressively with the enemy—Satan (James 4:7).

7. Wait in silent expectancy and then in obedience and faith utter what God brings to your mind (John 10:27).

8. Always have your Bible with you should God want to give you direction or confirmation from it (Psalm 119:105).

9. When God ceases to bring things to your mind to pray for, finish by praising and thanking Him for what He has done (Romans 11:36).

10. Be very careful with whom you may share whatever you believe God may have revealed to you (Luke 9:36).[89]

---

89   Joy Dawson, *How to Intercede Effectively*. Revival Prayer Focus, September/October 1979, 7.

Jesus said that we "should always pray and not give up" (Luke 18:1). To emphasize the point, He told a story of a confrontation between a desperate widow and a heartless judge (Luke 18:1–8). The widow won in the end because of the persistence of her pleading.

> Future history is shaped by intercessors who persist.

Future history is shaped by intercessors who persist.

Persistence Is the Key

In 1923, teenager Helen Malhenkof attended a Keswick Conference in New Jersey, USA. A speaker, L.L. Legters, challenged the young attendees to pray for different language groups in Mexico. Helen chose the Mazahua people. She wrote their name in the flyleaf of her Bible and promised the Lord she would pray for them daily, till they had a Bible in their own language.

Helen trained to become a nurse and worked for 35 years in India as a member of the Women's Union Missionary Society. In 1967 she retired to Lancaster, Pennsylvania. Shortly thereafter, for reasons unknown, she felt free to release herself from her commitment to pray daily for the Mazahua people.

In 1981, she read a newspaper report of how Pat Hamric, Hazel Spotts and Don and Shirley Stewart had been Wycliffe Bible translators among the Mazahua people. Through contact with them, she learned that the printed Bible had been dedicated to the Mazahua in 1970. This was the year in which the Lord had released her from the intercessory burden. For 48 years she had prayed the project through to completion.[90]

---

90   Bernie May, *Long-term Obedience*. Word Alive, Wycliffe, February/March 1991.

In 1944, when Korea was under Japanese occupation, God gave a vision to a Korean lady. It was of a special church that was to come into existence in the city of Seoul. For 20 years she interceded on behalf of that church, till it started to become a physical reality in

> **Only when we have knelt before God can we stand before others.**

1964. As surely as Simeon and Anna knew that the eight days old child before them, would be the long-awaited Messiah of Israel (Luke 2:25–29), this lady saw that Yoido Full Gospel Central Church would become the largest church in the world (pastored by Yonggi Cho). Her faithful persistent intercession over the decades prayed it into existence.

On March 20, 2022, Dutch Sheets, who leads an internationally recognized prayer ministry, issued a call for intercession to reverse what he perceived as the moral, political, financial and military decline of the USA. In his call he said,

> Actions, prayers and decrees, faith, endurance, obedience and more, are necessary in order to receive the fulfillment of God's will and promises… Satan tries to wear down the saints (Daniel 7:25) through discouragement, confusion and more… He tries to make us weary and cause us to lose heart (Galatians 6:9) …to distract us through the cares of life (and) business… But our prayers are transforming the nation and shaping history… This is not a time for 'business as usual'… We must take action… If we don't another generation could be lost.[91]

Intercession is being aware of the battlefield for the lives of people throughout the world and entering that battle,

---

91   *Dutch Sheets Appeals to Intercessors: Wake Up and Pray for America.* https://www.charismanews.com/video/88675-dutch-sheets-appeals-to-intercessors-wake-up-and-pray-for-america, March 20, 2022 (viewed March 22, 2022).

convinced that final victory belongs to Jesus. Satan fears nothing from prayerless study, prayerless work and prayerless religion. He probably isn't even overly concerned about books written about prayer such as this one. He may laugh at our toil and mock our much-vaunted human wisdom. But he trembles when he sees the weakest of us on our knees, interceding with God to implore that His will be done on earth as it is in heaven.

It's Our Time

Only when we have knelt before God can we stand before others. If the much-weakened church of the West is ever to get on its feet again, it must first sink to its knees. It is time for intercessors to arise, to take the lead on behalf of us all, to release the least used but most needed power of intercession before the throne of God.

Chapter 8
INTO BATTLE

The desert never sleeps and your flesh is
very much alive. Prepare yourself for battle.
Surrounding you are enemies that never rest.

Thomas à Kempis (1380-1471)

A United States chaplain had been ministering among military personnel in Germany for many years. Positive results were few and far between. He was eventually transferred to South Korea to work among US forces stationed in that country. Here he continued to minister, using the same methods and messages he had used in Germany. However, there was a surprisingly different outcome. Many of the troops committed to his care, for the first times in their lives, found Jesus as their Savior. How can the difference in responsiveness be explained?

The Koreans claim that every town and city has its own god. To break the spiritual power of these gods, every inch of territory must be fought for till victory is obtained. This is done through corporate prayer meetings on site in churches daily from 5am-6:30am and throughout each Friday night till 6:00am Saturday. Additionally, each church member goes out to their church's respective prayer mountains to pray for a minimum of three days a year.[92]

Lilias Trotter (1853-1928) served as a missionary in Algeria for 40 years till her death. In a letter to Dr Samuel Zwemer

---

92   Paul Yonggi Cho, *Prayer*. Sermon preached at Garden City Church Conference, Brisbane, March 1985.

(1867-1952) who worked on the Arabian Peninsula and who was known as an "Apostle to Islam", she described an event in the life of a convert from Islam.

The young man came from a well-respected family. He had made good progress in understanding and practicing his new faith as a disciple of Jesus. Suddenly, the missionaries lost all contact with him. He seemed to have disappeared. Without further knowledge of what may have happened or contact with him, the missionaries continued to pray for him.

To prepare for the forthcoming winter season, as workers were clearing out the fireplace in the mission house, they found a small piece of paper with the young man's name written on it. It was retrieved and carefully smoothed out. Having deciphered what else was written on the paper, it proved to be a charm. Its purpose was to prevent the new believer from ever visiting the mission house again or his having anything to do with the missionaries.

The missionaries, calling on the name of Jesus, prayed to break the curse of the spell cast over the young man. They then burnt the paper. Within an hour the new believer returned. He confessed his backsliding and asked for forgiveness. Later he told the missionaries that he thought he must have been drugged, because he had suddenly developed a hatred for them or the thought of ever coming near to their house again.[93]

How would we interpret such an event in our Western culture?

Pastor Jim Cymbala and his wife Carol were devastated. For years they had basked in God's blessing as he had built the Brooklyn Tabernacle through their ministry in New York. But then their eldest daughter, Chrissy, who had been a model child, started to stray away from the family and God. As parents

---

93   Miriam Huffman Rockness, *A Passion for the Impossible–the Life of Lilias Trotter.* Grand Rapids Michigan, Discovery House Publishers, 2003, 232-233.

they tried everything to restrain and restore their daughter. At age 18, as soon as she was legally entitled to do so, Chrissy left home. When Carol was recovering from an operation, a hysterectomy, she felt the Devil say to her, "...You and your husband can go ahead to reach the world for Christ–but I'm going to have your children. I've already got the first one. I'm coming for the next two."

Devoid of any other means of influence over their daughter, having lost all contact, the only option left for Pastor Jim and Carol was to continue to pray fervently for their daughter. They also prayed that Satan would not succeed in any of his plans for their other children.

For two and a half years, emotional and spiritual turmoil gripped the family. Then during a Tuesday night prayer meeting at the church, a lady had a note passed through to Pastor Jim. She felt that the meeting needed to be stopped and all present should join in praying for the Pastor's daughter. Across the sanctuary everyone joined hands and began to pray. There arose a groaning, a sense of desperate determination, as if to say, "Satan, you will not have this girl. Take your hands off her– she is coming back!"

The spiritual force in the meeting almost knocked Pastor Jim over. He returned home to tell his wife that he believed that their "nightmare" involving Chrissy was over.

Thirty-two hours later, Chrissy returned home and begged for forgiveness from God and her parents, for what she had done. The she said, "On Tuesday night–who was praying for me? In the middle of the night, God woke me and showed me I was heading for an abyss. There was no bottom to it–it scared me to death... But at the same time... God wrapped His arms around me and held me tight. He kept me from sliding further and He said, 'I still love you.'"

Chrissy went on to enroll in a Bible College. She became a pastor's wife and had three children of her own.[94]

What's the element common to these events in Germany, Korea, Algeria and the United States?

The Common Element–Spiritual Warfare

During the 2022 Academy Awards presentation for the movie industry, Will Smith had a "brain snap". Comedian Chris Rock, Master of Ceremonies for the occasion, had made insensitive comments about Smith's wife, Jada Pinkett-Smith. Suffering from the autoimmune condition, alopecia, she had lost most of her hair. Smith, incensed at Rock's comments, walked onto the stage and slapped him across the face.

A short while later, a somewhat chastened Smith, returned to the stage to receive his "best actor" Academy Award. He told the worldwide audience that following his previous impromptu episode, Denzel Washington, an even more famous actor-celebrity, had come to him and said, "At your highest moment, be careful. That's when the Devil comes for you."

What did Washington mean by that comment?

Elsewhere, previously he had expressed the view, that the temptation towards fame and self-centeredness, is part of an ongoing spiritual battle. In an interview with a New York Times journalist, he reportedly described the process as "spiritual warfare."[95] It seems that the worldview and conclusions of a Hollywood actor may be more Biblical than that held by many Western Christians.

---

94   Jim Cymbala, *Fresh Wind, Fresh Fire*. Grand rapids, Michigan, Zondervan, 1977, 59 & 66.

95   Rebecca Abbot, *The Source of Denzel Washington's Advice to Will Smith*. https://www.eternitynews.com.au/current/the-source-of-denzel-washingtons-advice-to-will-smith/ March 29, 2022 (viewed April 1, 2022).

Do Satan and Hell Exist?

When it comes to discussing matters relating to Satan, demons, deliverance and hell, there are two common errors. The first is to disbelieve in their existence, or if they exist, they are only operating in regions not yet Christianized and industrialized. In this, we arrogantly assume that there could be no demonic activity in economically advanced affluent nations. That possibility is relegated to far off more "primitive" cultures.

Long ago, Charles Beaudelaire (1821–1867) advised that the Devil's best ruse was to persuade us that he doesn't exist. If that is so, Satan would seem to have crafted a winning strategy. According to a cover article in an Australian national news magazine, *The Bulletin*, decades ago the trend of disbelief about Satan and his horde was well entrenched. The article was entitled, *A consumer's guide to Hell*. While 79.4% of Australians still believed in God and 57.6% believed in heaven, only 39% believed in Hell. Advocates for the comforting syncretism of secularism were increasingly diluting Christian theology. In the same article, Dr Graeme Ferguson, principal of the United Theological College was quoted as saying, "You are in an intolerable situation if you think those who believe in Jesus Christ and those who don't are different."[96]

In the next decade, Australia's richest man at that time, Kerry Packer, "died" and was revived. After this experience he was quoted as saying, "Do you want the good news or the bad news? The good news is there's no Devil. The bad news is there's no heaven. There's nothing."[97] Undoubtedly this may have resulted in a sigh of relief across secular post-Christian Australia.

Another decade further on, the trend in the West continued. A lengthy report in the *Los Angeles Times* claimed that, "Hell is

---

96   Jen Corbett, Jan McGuiness, *A consumer's guide to Hell.* The Bulletin, May 24, 1988, 42-49.

97   Kerry Packer, *On God.* The Australian, February 17, 1995, 10.

being frozen out by many preachers who downplay damnation in their sermons... as a result of the influence of secularism on (their) Christian theology." Bruce Shelley, at that time a senior professor of Church History at Denver Theological Seminary, explained that the reason for the shift away from traditional teaching was, "because concepts of Satan and Hell were just too negative... Churches are under enormous pressure to be consumer-oriented. Churches today feel the need to be appealing rather than demanding."[98]

The oft-quoted prophecy made by General William Booth, founder of the Salvation Army, may have come true. He said, "The chief danger in the twentieth century will be religion without the Holy Ghost, Christianity without Christ, forgiveness without repentance, salvation without regeneration, politics without God and Heaven without Hell."[99]

There would be widespread agreement that much of Booth's prophecy is applicable to 21st century Western Christianity as well.

The other common mistake is to attribute every unfortunate, disagreeable, negative event or experience as an outcome of demonic activity. A mantra of many comedians in mid-twentieth century America was, "The debil made me do it." That line always got a good laugh. But within humorous comments there are often hidden truths to disarm the unwary. Commenting on the state of Christianity in America at the beginning of the twentieth century, evangelist Billy Sunday (1862–1935) declared, "If there is no hell, a good many preachers are obtaining money under false pretenses."[100]

---

98   *Hell 'frozen out' of preachers' sermons.* Charisma News Service, June 19, 2002.
99   Francis Dixon. Words of Life Ministries Newsletter, Summer 1990.
100 Larry Dixon, *Whatever happened to Hell?* Moody, June 1993, 26.

Jesus Believed

It's difficult to explain away the realities of Satan, demons and hell, because Jesus Himself gave them such prominence, in both His practice of ministry and teaching His disciples. In the last major teaching discourse before His betrayal, trial and execution, He majored on these very issues.

He spoke of wrath, of sheep and goats, of the Devil, of demons and of a fiery place (Matthew 25:31-46). He likened those who rejected His message to be as weeds incinerated in a fire (Matthew 13:40, 13:48). Hell meant to be utterly separated from God (Matthew 7:23), a place of darkness and agony (Matthew 8:12), where there was a fiery furnace full of people weeping and wailing, gnashing their teeth in agony (Matthew 13:42, 50). From that place, there would be neither relief nor way of escape (Luke 16:23-26).

Despite all the Biblical and contemporary evidence, many Western Christians continue to speak and act as if that to which Denzel Washington referred, "spiritual warfare", is at best a side issue or a myth of the ancient world, that has no place in our knowledge-based contemporary worldview.

Flawed Thinking

Missiologists call this phenomenon, the "flaw of the excluded middle." They conclude that in the West, we see only a two-tiered universe. Tier one consists of the visible things of this world. Tier two consists of the invisible things of the other world where God exists. That which is excluded is what exists between these two tiers, namely the invisible things of this world—the realm of angels, demons, deliverance and the spiritual battle in which we are knowingly or unknowingly all involved.[101] In this we are either passive instruments, "useful idiots", or tools to be exploited and deployed at Satan's whim. Alternatively, we

---

101   Kurt Mahlburg, Warwick Marsh, *Power of Prayer*. Unanderra, NSW, Australian Heart Publishing, 2021, 107.

are fully cognizant, engaged and active on God's behalf in this battle of the ages, to facilitate God's will being done on earth as it is in heaven.

A Canadian organization, *Thunder and Light Studios*, seeks to provide online resources for any wanting to grow in understanding and practice of Spiritual Warfare. They identify three contemporary widespread misconceptions that detract from effectiveness in this area:

1. Spiritual warfare is only for professionals.
   This belief has stopped many in the church from becoming the warriors they are called to be.

2. Satan and demons are a myth or just symbolic of evil.
   Satan is real, organized and has an army of fallen angels at his command.

3. This stuff is too scary and we shouldn't mess with it.[102]

Whether we want to believe it or not, we are in a battle.

Thunder and Light's material highlights some of Jesus and Paul's teaching on the subject. They are right to do so when we remember that our highest authority on these matters, Jesus, spoke about hell, judgment and punishment more than any other person referred to as a source in the Biblical record. It has been calculated that 13% of His teaching and half of His parables related to this matter. So why do we try to avoid it or disbelieve in those realities?

Commenting on the need to enter the spiritual battle via prayer, Leonard Ravenhill (1907-1994), well-known author of a previous generation, profiled the community of believers as follows:

> We have many organizers, but few agonizers.
> We have many players, but few prayers.

---

102   *We are all facing battle*. Thunder and Light Studios, Calgary, Canada, April 7, 2022.

We have many singers, but few clingers.
We have many members, but few wrestlers.
We have many fears, but few tears.
We have many fashions, but little passion.
We have many interferers, but few intercessors.
We have many writers, but few fighters.[103]

All of that may be true, but it doesn't need to remain like that. If all believers are already in the army of the Lord, we need to start to report for duty as the call goes out. But before we enter this conflict, we need to familiarize ourselves with the weapons of our warfare.

Weapons of Warfare

Ephesians 6:10-18 provides the most comprehensive list detailing what is available for our use. In the list given to us by Paul, the first five items are for defensive purposes. These include:

- The Belt of truth.
- The Breastplate of righteousness.
- Footwear of the Gospel of peace.
- The Shield of faith.
- The Helmet of salvation.

1. Word of God

Suited up for protection, the believer only then is provided with the first weapon with which to launch an attack—the Sword, the Word of God.

"If you want to put Satan to flight... the weapon we must use is the weapon of attack... the sword of the Spirit, which is the Word of God."[104] This is precisely what Jesus did in His encounter with Satan (Matthew 4:1-11).

---

103 Stuart Robinson, *Spiritual Warfare-Prayer.* Blackburn Baptist Church Bulletin, October 25, 1987.
104 Derek Prince, *Secrets of a Prayer Warrior.* Grand Rapids, Michigan, Chosen, 2009, 137.

> The delivery system for the weapons listed in Ephesians 6, "Pray in the Spirit on all occasions… Be alert and always keep on praying…

The Apostle Paul reminds us that, "the weapons we fight with are not the weapons of the world. On the contrary, they have divine power to demolish strongholds" (2 Corinthians 10:4). It's as if they come in special packaging labeled, "Danger. Handle with care."

The delivery system for the weapons listed in Ephesians 6, appears right at the end—prayer. "Pray in the Spirit on all occasions… Be alert and always keep on praying… Pray for me also" (Ephesians 6:18-19). We are assured that our prayers are powerful and effective (James 5:16).

In addition to all the above, there are other weapons at our disposal.

2. Name of Jesus

Jesus said, "Until now you have not asked for anything in My name. Ask and you will receive, and your joy will be complete" (John 16:24).

In whose name we come is important. Satan and his minions have little fear of us. We are relative nobodies compared with our Commander-in-Chief, Jesus. He is Lord of all and it is "at the name of Jesus every knee shall bow" (Philippians 2:10). He is the supreme authority. This same Jesus said, "I have given you authority" (Luke 10:19). "I have given you the keys of the kingdom" (Matthew 16:19). The responsibility has been passed to us to engage.

3. Blood of Jesus

Not only is it through His blood that we have received redemption and forgiveness of sins (Ephesians 1:7), but it is by His blood that Satan is ultimately completely overcome (Revelation 12:11).

4. Praise

The ancient Israelites understood that God is enthroned or inhabits the praises of His people (Psalm 22:3). In their wanderings, His presence was represented by the Ark of the Covenant. It was briefly captured by the Philistines (1 Samuel 4) and that spelled disaster. When Israel's leading Priest, Eli, heard the news, the shock of it and the ramifications, resulted in his instant death. His daughter-in-law interpreted the event saying, "The glory has departed" (1 Samuel 4:21). Without God in their midst, they knew all was lost.

By the time of Jesus, God's presence was represented by the Holy of Holies in the Jerusalem Temple. This was the place in which God was to be worshiped. But when Jesus arrived on the scene, at first He was grieved and then angered. He interrupted trade, overturned tables and scattered the money-changers' coins across the cobblestones.

> What Jesus did in the Jerusalem Temple needs to be repeated in our own lives.

He called out, "It is written,... My house will be called a house of prayer, but you are making it a den of robbers" (Matthew 21:12-13).

Today according to 1 Corinthians 3:12-17, believers are now the Temple of God. In us the Spirit dwells. He desires to do amazing things through us (Ephesians 3:20). Unfortunately, our "temples" are also polluted by sin and focused on "business as usual". We sing that we want to be A *People of Power*, but for that to become a reality what may be required? What Jesus did in the Jerusalem Temple needs to be repeated in our own lives.

> a. Jesus cleansed the Temple so that it became **PURE** (vs. 12).
>
> b. He announced it to be a place of **PRAYER** (vs. 13).
>
> c. It was then transformed into a place of **POWER** (vs.14).
>
> d. Only then did it become a place of **PRAISE** (vs.16).

Smelly oxen, bleating sheep, tarnished coins and "business as usual" are poor substitutes for the holy presence of God. The process exemplified by Jesus in the Jerusalem Temple, will probably need to be repeated if God in all His power is to dwell in the midst of our praises. Only then will our praise become an authentic statement of faith, declaring the victories of our God before they are attained.

Identify the "Strong Man"

It's also helpful to be able to identify specifically against whom we may be fighting. Referring to driving out demons by the Spirit of God, Jesus used the analogy of entering a strong man's house. He noted that before anything may be achieved, we need firstly to neutralize the strongman (Matthew 12:29).

To the Corinthian believers Paul said, "I do not fight like a man beating the air" (1 Corinthians 9:26). We are not to waste time on generalities. We need to wait upon God to understand better, the specifics of the forces that will oppose us.

As in Korea, so also in Argentina. Since the second half of the twentieth century the Evangelical/Pentecostal form of church has been growing exponentially. Like the Koreans, Argentinians also believe there are spiritual authorities over each town and city.

Before evangelist Omar Cabrera commences an outreach in any city, he and others spend time in prayer and fasting. Through this they can identify the spiritual powers that hold the territory in bondage. Only when they believe they have overcome the adverse spiritual dominance of a region, do they commence their proclamation of the Gospel. The results are extraordinary.

Cabrera says that unless they pray, fast and overcome before commencing, the outcome would be like laying on a banquet for prisoners inside a goal, with the banquet located outside the prison walls. In the overcrowded Argentinian penal system, inmates often hang out the barred windows, shouting, whistling, trying to attract the attention of passersby. They are free to do whatever they like inside the jail. But none of this enables their escape to attend the banquet set up outside.

Cabrera likens the Gospel he preaches to a similar banquet laid out for all who are imprisoned by their own sin. To participate, walls must come down. With prayer, fasting and revelation of who or what the local "strong man" is, using the authority delegated to believers, the walls are cast down. Only after this does Cabrera preach. Then people "drop" into the Kingdom of God like ripe fruit falling from a tree.

A Battle Plan

A comprehensive Biblical illustration of how weapons are used collectively in spiritual warfare is found in 2 Chronicles 20. Jehoshaphat, king of Judah, was facing certain defeat in battle. A vast coalition force of Moabites, Ammonites and Edomites was coming from the east. Jehoshaphat knew, that against such an overwhelming superior invading force, he had no hope humanly speaking. So, he moved the imminent battle from the physical to the spiritual realm. To snatch victory from the jaws of defeat, his battle plan had four steps.

1. He proclaimed a fast (2 Chronicles 20:3).
   This focused everyone's attention on the main issue at hand.

2. He united the people.
   Under his orders they came from every town "to seek help from the Lord" (2 Chronicles 20:4).
   To go into battle disunited is assuring defeat. Unity is an essential prerequisite for victory (Matthew 12:25).

3. He led the assembled troops in prayer.
   It wasn't just any prayer. He prayed based on the Word of God as much as was available to them. He reminded God that His interventions and promises had brought them to this place (2 Chronicles 20:5-12). These actions resulted in a spirit of prophecy coming upon Zechariah, the son of Beniah (vs.14-15).

4. Praise (v.19).
   The assembly was so encouraged, that initially there was a release of praise that became another weapon of warfare. Nothing could be as effective in driving spiritual opposition from the field of battle, as combined choirs preceding the army into battle singing "Praise the Lord, for His mercies endure forever" (v.21).

So much for the theory supported by Biblical history. How does this work out in contemporary practice?

From Theory to Practice

When Russia invaded Ukraine in 2022, President Putin was given to understand by his intelligence chiefs that there would be little resistance. Victory would be achieved quickly. He was dismayed to learn that nothing could be further from the truth. FSB intelligence chiefs, Sergey Beseda and Anatoly Bolyukh, were reportedly arrested. They were blamed for the embarrassing defeats of the Russian military in the opening weeks of war in the Ukraine.

Effective battle plans are always developed from good intelligence, collected from the field in which the battle will be fought. From this, down through the ranks, troops will be briefed to minimize any surprises or unknowns. It is not too dissimilar when preparing for spiritual encounters, skirmishes and battles.

Spiritual Mapping

A contemporary term used for this information gathering is "Spiritual Mapping". It is not a term used in the Bible. But there are many things not mentioned in the Bible that today we find useful—radio, television, computers, automobiles, Sunday School, closing our eyes when we pray, the title "Reverend" and much more. Spiritual mapping involves observation, interpretation and revelation. In this way, it is possible to develop an overlay of what may be the spiritual forces or influences operating in any given area. These will need to be specifically overcome through prayer.

Acts 17:16-34 provides clues as to the practical usefulness of such a process. Paul, upon arrival in Athens, had obviously completed a preliminary investigation of the territory and identified possible sources of opposition. Included in his list were idols, a synagogue, the marketplace, Epicurean and Stoic philosophers and their disputation tendencies, the Areopagus as the location for the clash of ideas, various other objects of worship including one to "An Unknown God". Not only did this provide content for the opening salvo of his first sermon, but it would also guide him toward the specifics of his intercessory prayers, for the people ensnared in this cauldron of competitive religious and philosophical concepts.

The results of his first message were admittedly meager. Only "a few became followers of Paul and believed" (Acts 17:34).

An area reportedly benefitting from implementing Biblical methodology with contemporary insights is Tillamook County in Oregon, USA.[105] Its 2880 square kilometers consist of lush dairy land, beautiful forests and sandy beaches bordered by majestic mountains. It appears to be ideally peaceful. However, beneath its serene surface a different picture emerges.

Reportedly, severe alcohol and drug abuse has been increasing. New Age practices, Wicca, alternative lifestyles and other movements have become more militant and persuasive in their influence over county affairs. Only 10% of inhabitants are associated with any church. All this has contributed toward the County being among America's least churched areas.

Against this background, a group of spiritual mappers— the field investigators—and intercessors, was birthed in 1997. Their goal was to uncover the spiritual DNA of the area. They did this through interviews, researching in local libraries and museums, reading minutes of town meetings, speaking with police, schoolteachers, farmers and students.

They reportedly found that the lifestyles of the first people, indigenous native Americans, had laid a foundation of immorality, bloodshed, idolatry and broken covenants. The later wave of immigrants, the Europeans, had continued these practices. Idolatry and shamanism had morphed into contemporary witchcraft and New Age practices.

As a profile was built and passed back to intercessors to pray, change started to occur. Newspapers highlighted corruption that had been uncovered in County agencies. Witchcraft sites were vacated. Two occult bookstores closed. Drug busts occurred. A dramatic unity among churches happened as Pastors came together to get to know one another. Church leaders, who did not share a vision of unified prayer, left. They were replaced by those who did. The transformation continues.

---

105 Holly Hastings, *The Road to Community Transformation.* World InSight, Lynnwood, WA, USA, Sentinel Group, February 2000, 6-7.

No one imagines transformation will be completed quickly. Every inch of territory will be contested. But the church, previously lulled into sleep, has awoken and joined the battle.

In the UK, Inspector Roger Bartlett was worried. The cleanup rate for crime detection in Barnstaple was one of the poorest in the region of Devon and Cornwall. Fatal road accidents were among the highest. So, Inspector Bartlett asked believers to pool their efforts in calling for back up from God. Results came quickly. Within three days a troublesome "prolific burglar" was apprehended. Within a year the unsolved crime detection rate dropped from 74% to 60%. Road fatalities decreased by 67%.[106]

In Brazil there was a far more serious problem. Sao Paulo was a city of 22 million people. Crime, corruption and poverty were endemic. Contributing to the problem was the out-of-control police force itself. Lieutenant Joel Rocha and Captain Alexander Terra decided to act.

Firstly, they met together weekly to pray over the state of their city and its police force. Next, they called on the 1,500 members of the Christian officers Association to join in, to start praying for their communities. Colonel Oswaldo Sorge was responsible for the area of Freguesia do O. In this area, homicides and massacres were commonplace as bandits operated with impunity. It was recognized as one of Sao Paulo's most dangerous areas. Families mostly stayed locked in their homes. They were too afraid even to allow their children to attend school. Police went to pastors, telling them they had failed in their responsibility to shepherd the area spiritually. The pastors repented, united, joined with the police and started to pray.

Officer Sorge asked God for wisdom, understanding and strategies to defeat what they faced. The first transformation

---

106   Beth Hale, *Police chief hails power of prayer in driving down town's crime rates.* Mail Online, http://www.dailymail.co.uk/news/article-1252708/Policeman-called-churchgoers-asking-for-prayer. February 22, 2010 (viewed February 27, 2010).

started within the police force. As evidence of that emerged, the public started to trust them more. Massive drug busts occurred. The murder rate fell by 60%. Christian officers and pastors visited families in crisis. Lives were changed. Marriages were restored. Children were delivered from drugs.

Sao Paulo's Police Academy began training officers in Biblical principles. Police commanders from other regions, learning of Sao Paulo's success, started to come to learn from it. Officer Rocha said, "Now I understand what God wants to do through us." Officer Sorge added, "I believe God changes history. God changes people. God transforms the hearts of people. I believe this because God changed my history."[107]

What happened in Sao Paulo was happening elsewhere in Brazil.

Cuiaba is a city of 700,000 people in Mato Grosso State. Its history was like elsewhere in the nation, as were the outcomes. Originally populated by indigenous Indians, this was followed by settlers from other countries: rangers, squatters and slaves. Poverty, corruption, child abuse and weak family life were typical. In the 1980s, Pastor Gisella Guth De Arango started a ministry of prayer, soup, soap and salvation. She led repentance for historic and contemporary bloodshed in the city, as she systematically prayer-walked the streets and all the favelas (slums) of Cuiaba.

In 2004 a new mayor was elected. He was shocked to learn that municipal salaries had been unpaid for three months and the city administration was in an acute terminal stage.

Desperate for help, he agreed to follow the advice of Pastor Gisella and five other pastors. This was that he confess the sins of the city since its foundation, seek forgiveness and

---

107   Stan Jeter, *Christian Police Transform Community Through God*. Worldwide Kingdom/Revival NEWS. http://www.openheaven.com/forums/forum-posts-asp?TID=32756, April 6, 2010, (viewed June 11, 2010).

reconciliation with God. The mayor prayed for over an hour. Within five days all salaries were paid and administration was back in order. This was publicly declared to be a miracle.

The mayor and his deputy conducted a public ceremony giving the keys of the city to Jesus. In more than 100 cities other mayors did likewise. By 2011 it was reported that drug trafficking was in decline. Police forces were being cleaned up. Evil powers were being expelled through prayer networks. Old covenants of spiritual significance were being revoked.[108]

Uruguay was known as South America's most secular nation. In 1998, 150 years after the arrival of the first Protestant missionary, there were still only 150 churches scattered across the nation. A combined prayer movement was initiated. By 2005 the number of evangelical churches had doubled to include up to 5% of the population in attendance.

During the same period a similar prayer movement was undertaken in Peru. Whereas the number of Evangelicals had been one percent of the national population, it quickly grew to number 10%.

When disciples are not taught how to pray, evangelism grows weaker.

In New Delhi, India, fasting, prayer walking, binding the powers of darkness and overcoming spiritual strongholds has become a normative practice. Whereas in one three-year period only 29 new churches had been commenced, following the more effective engagement at the spiritual warfare level, 181 churches were planted in the following two years.[109]

---

108 Gisella Guth De Arango, Joel News International 792, October 6, 2011.
109 Amaury Bragga et al, Joel News Service. http://www.openheaven.com/forums/printer-friendly-posts.asp?FID=3&TID-10353, June 6, 2006 (viewed July 8, 2006).

Peter Sekhonyane is based in Orange Farm, 50 kilometers south of Johannesburg in South Africa. He reported that in a six-year period, he saw 840,000 people come to Christ. How did this happen?

Peter was a concrete engineer called to be an evangelist and church planter. But having reached a crisis in his ministry, he considered returning to his secular profession. Before doing so, he locked himself away in a hotel room for a three-day personal retreat. He reported that during this time God rebuked him, saying he was doing the work, but not spending enough time with Him. Similarly, prayerless pastors were producing prayerless congregations. When disciples are not taught how to pray, evangelism grows weaker. He recommended his ministry by establishing a foundation of prayer.

During the following six years, he saw 7,800 prayer "watches" established in local churches. Teams engaged in prayer 24/7. They confronted the powers of darkness. 190 witch doctors came to faith. 246 marriages were restored. And hundreds of thousands of new believers entered the Kingdom of Heaven, as foundational prayer support increased to win the war in the heavenlies.[110]

But perhaps the best-documented regional spiritual transformation is what happened at Almolonga in Guatemala.

A Contemporary Miracle

Until five centuries ago Guatemala was the center of the ancient Mayan civilization. Then in the 15th century, the Spanish conquistadors arrived in the New World in their search for fabled gold and more territories to conquer. Up till then, the indigenous people had been worshipping the god Maximon.

---

110 Adrienne Gains, *South African Minister Credits 24-7 Prayer With 840,000 Salvations.* Worldwide Kingdom Revival NEWS. http://www.openheaven.com/forums/printer-friendly-posts.asp?FID-3&TID-32808, June 10, 2010 (viewed June 11, 2010).

The Spanish invaders brought with them Roman Catholicism and their veneration of the Madonna, Mary the mother of Jesus.

While the locals were forced to cede territorial sovereignty, one aspect of life they would not surrender—devotion to Maximon. The newcomers built their cathedrals and littered the landscape with their churches. They also sprinkled their holy water over the local population, declaring them now to be baptized into the new religion of Christianity. But the locals, forced to change externally, remained committed internally to Maximon.

They were unable to bring their images inside the sacred Catholic spaces, to place them alongside the foreign images already mounted there. So they disguised their worship by transferring their devotion, but not their allegiance, to the Catholic veneration of Saint Simon. In this way they could continue to bring their offerings and ask for favors and protection as before. Cigar smoking, alcohol drinking and immorality (from a Christian perspective) were widely associated with devotion to Maximon.

In the state of Quetzaitenango in a large valley in the highlands, a couple of hours west of the capital city, nestles the town of Almolonga. There, Quiché Indians made their covenants with Maximon and others of his associates, like Pascual Bailon, the Lord of Death. Spiritual forces, represented by the idols, held villages in bondage as they attempted mediation and manipulation through occult and witchcraft practices.

The result was that most males became alcoholics. This in turn led to widespread domestic violence and a high rate of incarceration in the four local jails. Ensuing poverty and corruption added to the overall misery of the local people. Education of children was neglected. Evangelists were chased away. Their churches were stoned.

After Pastor Mariono was physically attacked and threatened with death, he established evening prayer meetings. Christians started to pray desperately for God's intervention, to address the intolerably unbearable depths into which all had fallen.

One pastor, almost by accident, discovered their problems could be associated with demonic influence. When he prayed for an unconscious alcoholic who had beaten up his wife again, he was as surprised as was the drunkard, to find that upon regaining consciousness, the man was quite different. The transformed alcoholic soon surrendered his life to Jesus and began witnessing to his friends. They also became believers.

Later a powerful priest of the Maximon cult was dying. Nothing could cure him. When José Albina Tazel cried out to God to save him at 11:40pm, as he awoke from another drinking binge, he announced he had found freedom in Jesus. All the family idols and witchcraft paraphernalia were burned. Soon others were being delivered from demons associated with their idols. The church intensified intercessory prayer. José journeyed to the nearby mountains to fast, pray and seek God.

Theresa, a local woman, developed gangrene after a Caesarian Section. She died. Pastor Mariano was asked to conduct her funeral. Instead, he and his associate Valeriano, prayed and the woman came back to life completely healed. Many more gave their lives to Jesus.

Eventually, over 18,000 of the 20,000 Almolongans put their faith in Jesus. 81% of bars were converted into churches. Houses have been newly rebuilt in the now clean and prosperous town. Agricultural productivity has improved by 1,000%. Locals pay cash to buy trucks to transport their product from what has become known as the "Garden of the Americas". Locals say God has healed their land in terms of 2 Chronicles 7:14. Giant-sized highly prized vegetables are the result.

Literacy has improved. The divorce rate has been reduced to zero. Women have been elevated to play a significant role in the economic uplift of the community. The local brothel has been closed as have the four local jails. Police no longer carry guns. They blow whistles to unscramble traffic jams of locals' newly purchased vehicles. Stores are stocked with food rather than alcohol.

Christians continue to pray and fast every week to break any remaining spiritual strongholds. On the approach to the town a large sign proclaims, "Jesus is Lord of Almolonga".

Pastor Mariano says that to maintain the spiritual transformation that has occurred, God has provided a strategy:

1. Live in the fear of the Lord.
2. Maintain intense prayer and fasting.
3. Build Christian schools.
4. Care for new converts.
5. Establish strong families.[111]

Governments around the world, who repeatedly fail in their attempts to alleviate their societies of Almolonga-type conditions through legislation, money and law enforcement would do well to study the Almolonga example. But it would require great humility and courage to proceed along this path. Unfortunately, these traits are seldom in evidence anywhere in our various political systems.

To reverse a century of decline of Christianity in the West, we will need to acknowledge the worldwide reality of Spiritual Warfare.

111 Carol Saia, *God Ends Idol's 700-year Reign in Guatemalan Village*. Worldwide Kingdom/Revival NEWS. http://www.openheaven.com/forums/printer-friendly-posts.asp?FID=3&TID=34664, July 11, 2010 (viewed November 13, 2010).

So why is there this pile on of a multiplicity of examples from a single splice of history from various continental contexts? It's simply to draw attention to the fact that they are mostly from developing countries. There are, admittedly, a few from Western contexts, that at least demonstrate the proposition that spiritual warfare is a universal challenge.

But the most obvious results are seen outside the developed, articulate, erudite, "sophisticated", affluent, materialist Western world. There, many churches feel the need to be attractive rather than encouraging repentance and living under the Lordship of Jesus. In the developing world, often faith is simple. Obedience is immediate.

To reverse a century of decline of Christianity in the West, we will need to acknowledge the worldwide reality of Spiritual Warfare. Having done that, we need to take up our weapons and begin to fight. But to even hope of any chance of victory, we need to revert to the starting point that Jesus commended, to have the simple, uncluttered faith of a little child (Mark 10:15; Luke 18:17). Only then may we arise, unite and fight.

Chapter 9
THE LAST FRONTIER

*I have but one candle of life to burn
and would rather burn it put where
people are dying in darkness than
in a land flooded with light.*

—Anon

Eric Moore was the Project Coordinator for the new equipment being installed at Christian Radio Station HCJB. The work site was in Papallacto, Ecuador. Eric lived 30 kilometers distant in Fifo.

It had been a busy day conferring with colleagues, checking progress on various aspects of the project, taking important phone calls and detailing work for the contractors to undertake the next day. Night was approaching as Eric finally started up his vehicle for the drive home. The road was narrow and winding. Few others used it after dark. It crossed the Andes Mountain range at an altitude of 4,114 meters (13,500 feet).

Because of the frequency with which Eric drove this route, he knew every twist and turn, pothole and washout along the way. He could almost drive it with his eyes closed. But suddenly, the vehicle lurched and in the next instant Eric found himself off the road rolling down the mountain side. When the vehicle finally stopped, Eric realized he was now in great danger. He was unable to free himself because his leg was pinned under the vehicle. Not only that, with fuel dripping from the somersaulted

> The origins of the missionary movement are the result of Jesus' example and teaching.

vehicle and its engine still hot, the whole lot could explode in a ball of flame at any instant.

Eric had cause for concern. If fire didn't kill him then blood loss might. Added to all that, there was the exposure to the high altitude's falling temperature and the isolation of the road. Even if another vehicle did come by, there was little chance Eric would be seen down the side of the mountain.

However, at exactly that time far away in Ireland, some folk in Eric's home church were meeting for their regular Bible study. One of those present interrupted the flow of the meeting, to say they felt burdened to pray for the Moores in Ecuador— right now. The group agreed. All joined in praying for whatever might be the need on the other side of the world.

Back in the Andes mountains, something caught the eye of a passing motorist. He stopped to investigate. From where he was on the side of the road, he could just make out Eric's vehicle down the slope. Eric was found and rescued.

Later when stories were shared, it was discovered that the time of the accident in Ecuador, was the same time the people in Ireland had been urged to pray. Those timely prayers were heard and answered.

Missionaries

Eric is one of those who shared in a long tradition of much maligned Christian workers known as "missionaries". One jester defined them as the only people who teach cannibals to say grace before they eat them! At least the element of self-sacrifice was correct. The word "missionary" has the same meaning as the word "apostle". They both mean *"one who is sent forth"*. "Missionary" is based on ancient Latin language. "Apostle" is based upon Greek.

The origins of the missionary movement are the result of Jesus' example and teaching. This is most succinctly expressed in what is known as the Great Commission. This was given among the last commands of our Lord before His ascension. In different forms, this commission is recorded in each of the Gospels and in the Acts of the Apostles.

In Latin there is a saying descriptive of a common learning process—"repetitio mater studiorum." Literally it translates as *"repetition is the mother of learning or study."* Colloquially it might be better understood as, "throw mud at a brick wall long enough and some of it might stick!"

Clearly if the Holy Spirit caused something to be recorded five times, we were not meant therefore, to forget or overlook its significance.

Great Commissions

In Matthew 28:19-20 Jesus said, "…go and make disciples of all nations, baptising them in the name of the Father and of the Son and of the Holy Spirit and teaching them to obey everything I have commanded you." The key verb in this passage upon which all else depends is "make disciples". This indicates the **DEPTH** of the commission.

In Mark 16:15 Jesus said, "Go into all the world and preach the good news to all creation." This indicates the **WIDTH** of the commission. The message was to be taken to "all the world… to all creation."

In Luke 24:45-48 Jesus revealed the significance of His death and resurrection and its relationship to repentance and forgiveness of sin. This gives us our understanding or **CONTENT** of the commission.

In John 20:21 Jesus said, "Peace be with you! As the Father has sent Me, I am sending you." He said this as He showed them His hands and side (v.20). In effect He was saying, "Look at Me. As the Father has sent Me and this has happened to Me, I am likewise sending you and you should expect the same to happen to you." This is the **COST** of the commission. Threaded through His teaching the same warning had often been given previously.

Acts 1:8 tells us the **SCOPE** of the commission beginning "in Jerusalem" and ending when it is implemented "to the ends of the earth."

> Given the rapid growth and geographical spread of the Christian faith in the first three centuries of its existence, despite severe persecution, as Jesus had forewarned in John 15:18-20, obviously those early disciples were making Jesus' last command their first priority.[112]

Roman Emperor Constantine's Edict of Milan in the year 313, granted religious liberty throughout the empire. This was followed in 321 by his legalization of bequests made to Christian churches. This transformed Christianity from being a "religio illicita," that which was alien to and subversive of the State, to being officially accepted by the State. Change came quickly.

Physical buildings came to express authority. That was associated with clergy being ranked within hierarchies. But compared with earlier centuries, as the church turned to focus on internal matters, its rate of outward expansion slowed. Vast continents were left unreached.

Delayed Revelation

Many centuries later, in Europe in the sixteenth century, at the time of what became known as the Protestant Reformation,

---

112   Stuart Robinson, *Daring to Disciple*. Upper Mt Gravatt, Brisbane, CHI Books, 2020, 5.

many Biblical principles were recovered. But the imperative of cross-cultural mission was not one of them.

Leading Reformation theologian of the time, John Calvin (1509-1564), is quoted as saying that the Gospel does not fall from the clouds like rain by accident. It is brought by the hands of those to whom God sent it. True. But the implications of his statement were neutralized, by the emphasis of his theology that stressed the sovereignty of God and predestination.

So persuasive was this thinking that centuries later, when Baptist Pastor William Carey (1761-1834), raised the question of mission to the "heathen", his fellow Baptist clergy advised him that God would do it in his own way and time. Carey resisted that prevailing view and sailed for India in 1793. He remained there till his death in 1834. For his 41 years of uninterrupted prodigious output, based inland from Kolkata in today's West Bengal, he has been described as the "father of modern missions."[113]

European theologian, Emil Brunner (1889-1966), aptly expressed the view that the church exists by mission as fire exists by burning. Therefore, that being so, if the church's passion and priority for evangelism, mission and outreach wanes, it ceases to be fully church. It no longer manufactures its own spiritual blood cells and becomes set on a path of decline and death, caused by a type of spiritual leukemia. In failing to face outward it turns inward. It preaches to the same people every week. Its continued existence then depends upon how well they entertain themselves.

Consumer Conditioning

Irrespective of congregational size, in practice that seems to represent much of the consumer-conditioned church of the West. In our society it's common for believers to float between

---

113   Justo L. Gonzalez, *The Story of Christianity, Vol.2: The Reformation to the Present Day*. Grand Rapids, MI, Zondervan, 2010, 419.

locations, sampling the best speakers who preach the most positively encouraging messages, supported by the best technology and music. That is to be enjoyed till a new and even more exciting, innovative presentation proves to be more alluring.

Preachers who attract the largest following, are often those who preach that God wants us to reach our full potential, to live our best lives in the here and now. That seems oddly at variance with the example and teaching of Jesus. He said, "I tell you the truth, unless a kernel of wheat falls into the ground and dies, it remains only a single seed. But if it dies, it produces many seeds... Whoever serves Me must follow Me" (John 12:24-26).

One of the reasons for Western Christianity's continuous decline through most of the twentieth century and up to the present day, is that too few have responded to the challenge of Jesus to "live dead". Only through such sacrificial "death" will multiplying seeds be reproduced.

One of the reasons Islam has continuously outpaced Christianity during the same period, lies in the oft quoted assertion, "We Muslims love death more than you Christians love life." They repeatedly tragically prove it by being willing to die on jihad—Holy War in the cause of Allah. Each death is celebrated by the community to which each belonged. Parents are honored for raising another shahid or *martyr*. Civil authorities pay special pensions for the remainder of the lives of dependents.

Protective Pastors

Meanwhile in the Christian community, it is unlikely that possible mission candidates will even hear of the call to missions. Many pastors are reluctant to permit a missionary advocate to present the case, for fear of losing a member or some finance to a cause outside of their local church.

Should a young candidate emerge, progress toward implementing a call to missions will often be resisted by parents and the local church. Furthermore, should that call be to one of the neediest places on the planet, where people are most resistant to the Christian message and peace may not be the guaranteed order of the day, even missionary agencies from the most affluent countries will resist assigning missionary candidates to those regions. Those who do go to share the Gospel in these regions, are frequently lambasted as reckless, careless individuals who are to be shunned, lest the safety and security of others be compromised.

Less than one percent of resources are allocated to still unreached people groups.

Numerous surveys over the decades, show we continue to spend more than 90% of our resources on ourselves. And even within that set aside for cross-cultural mission endeavor, less than one percent of resources are allocated to still unreached people groups (UPGs).

Cancelled Commissions

Many who claim to be Biblical in their operations fall into this category. Not only does the Great Commission remain unfulfilled because of our bias, but we deny what God Himself clearly desires. He sacrificed His Son to open the door of salvation to the whole world according to that most quoted verse of John 3:16. To clarify God's priorities further, elsewhere we read in the Bible that He is "not wanting anyone to perish, but everyone to come to repentance." (2 Peter 3:9). He wants everyone to be saved and to come to a knowledge of the truth (1 Timothy 2:4). So how are we to cut our way free from the self-protective layers of security netting within which we have become enmeshed?

Like everything else, to change church reluctance to engage, to be willing to release the finest and fittest candidates and to support them financially, all starts with focused prayer. As usual Jesus was aware of the problem long ago. Admittedly all the contemporary excuses we invent to explain away our failure to participate may not have been relevant in His time. Nevertheless the situation in which He found Himself, has remarkable similarities to our own in the Western world.

There existed a highly educated, financially secure, entitled, religious class of leadership. They focused upon maintaining the status quo and retaining all hard-won privileges which secured their institutions, their status in society and their own unchallenged futures. They turned inward, intent on domestic issues such as doctrinal disputes, the winning of which was essential in order to avoid heresy or any threat to moral rectitude. Contamination by association with secular authorities, those who were on the socio/religious blacklist for whatever reason, the red-light ladies, collaborators with infidels, and so on, was to be avoided at all costs.

Jesus on the other hand, with a different attitude, took a different path. He consorted with the marginalized, visited with the outcasts and even engaged with the rank, unbelieving, sinful class. And as for the opposite sex.... While the male religious elite of the day prayed, thanking God that they were not born as a woman or a dog, Jesus welcomed females amongst His disciples. He had meals with them. Those cast out for ritual reasons of disease or death, He healed. In fact, He disrupted every funeral in which He was involved, by bringing the dead back to life!

Plentiful Harvest

So, when He was confronted with a crowd who relentlessly followed and encircled Him, longing for healing, help and hope, He did not disappoint, seek to avoid or hold back.

> "When He saw the crowds, He had compassion on them, BECAUSE they were harassed and helpless, like sheep without a shepherd. Then He said to His disciples, 'The harvest is plentiful, but the workers are few. Ask (Pray) the Lord of the harvest, therefore, to send out workers into the harvest field'" (Matthew 9:36-38).

"The harvest is plentiful" was Jesus' interpretation of the scene which confronted Him. The condition of the human heart is unchanged. The longing for fulfilment and completion by reconnection with the Creator, is still the same for all of us. We may not recognize or understand that we need that which Jesus offers. The various community leaders, like those in Jesus' time, will certainly be hostile toward any defection to another religious identity, lest their power and position be threatened.

Altered Attitudes

We then persuade ourselves, that the assignment to reach these people is too difficult, too dangerous, if not impossible. We base our conclusions upon multiple stories from the past that testify to such failure and amplify similar outcomes with each retelling. We forget that "nothing is impossible with God" (Luke 1:37). So, we settle on the comforting concept of faithfulness, rather than wrestle with the disturbing outcome of fruitlessness.

It's easy to continue to do today what we did yesterday. That will ensure the same results tomorrow. In such cases we need to ask, "What are we doing or not doing, that prevents God doing what He wants to happen?" His desire is clear. He loves the whole of His creation and He wants everyone to be reconciled with Him (Romans 5:6-8).

The evidence is overwhelming. Where workers have courageously confronted a history of failure and adopted dramatically different approaches, positive results have followed. The harvest is still plentiful even in the most unlikely fields. To that I can testify from personal experience as a missionary in the South Asian context, as well as in the aggressively hostile, secularized nation of Australia.

Harvesting Harvesters

Having honestly assessed the situation, the next challenge to be faced is how to find and release workers into the harvest field where they are so needed? In answer to this, Jesus said we are to ask or pray to the Lord of the harvest to send out the workers. This is one prayer which is certain to be answered in the affirmative because, "...if we ask anything according to His will, He hears us. And if we know that He hears us—whatever we ask—we know that we have what we asked of Him" (1 John 5:14-15).

There is no doubt about God's will in this matter. Nor can there be any doubt about His response.

In 1784, the Northampton (UK) Baptist Association issued a call for regular concerted prayer. One of the objects of the prayer, was for "the spread of the Gospel to the most distant parts of the habitable globe."[114] This was "the springhead—the primary cause of the missionary excitement in (William) Carey's mind, and its diffusion among the Northampton ministers."[115] His response resulted in the formation of a society in 1792, "for the Propagation of the Gospel among the Heathen." This morphed into the Baptist Missionary Society. Later Congregationalists

---

114   Circular letter of the Northampton (Baptist) Association, 1784.

115   F.A. Cox, *History of the Baptist Mission, Vol.1.* London, T. Ward & Co. and G & J Dyer, 1842, 10.

were inspired to form the London Missionary Society in 1814. It also influenced the birth of other missionary societies in America, Holland, Switzerland and Germany.

Priority of Prayer

In continental Europe, because of an astonishing 100-year-long continuous prayer meeting among Moravians in Herrnhut, Germany, more than 100 missionaries were commissioned and constantly supported in prayer during 1727–1752.

In a church of which I was the founding pastor, in a 25-year period, we commissioned more than 100 missionaries as we prioritized prayer. This is the pattern for any who would aspire to become a Great Commission church. It should not surprise us. It has been thus from the very beginning.

In the church at Antioch, while believers were worshipping and praying, the Holy Spirit identified Barnabas and Saul. They were to be set aside, to become the first candidates called to leave the relative security of the believers' community. They were accordingly commissioned to initiate the adventure of cross-cultural evangelism, disciple-making and church planting on foreign soil.

Nothing less than the presence of the Holy Spirit will dispel our torpor, identify His privileged chosen ones and thrust them forth into the harvest. This is the effect of the spiritual power that is unleashed as we begin to pray to identify the workers.

The verb translated from Greek into English "to send out" in Matthew 9:38, is the same as in the next verse in Matthew 10:1. There it is translated as "to drive out" with reference to evil spirits. Regardless of the objects of the operation—harvester workers or evil spirits—the process is similar. Pray. Spiritual power deployed. Objective achieved.

Identifying Missionaries

At Antioch where the missionary movement originated, the candidates did not initiate the process. Nor were they isolated and instructed to go it alone. The Spirit spoke into the midst of the gathered community. The candidates did not self-select. It was after the believers continued for a period of extended fasting and prayer, that the impulse was confirmed as being from the Lord. Then hands were placed upon them in an act of commissioning and blessing. Only then were they sent off.

Unfortunately, in contemporary Western culture, we are stripped of the sense of community and identity. We live in individualized, siloed isolation. The effect of that is that local leadership no longer appreciates their responsibility to identify, encourage, equip and support the ones whom the Lord may well be calling. Silenced by our ever-intrusive privacy laws, we are reluctant to approach another with what may be a word from God. That might be considered an intrusion or invasion of another's privacy and therefore most unwelcome, if not illegal. Hence immature, inexperienced young adults are left to struggle alone, bereft of wisdom already available within their community of believers. Only God knows how many potential harvesters have been lost, because of their ignorance of how to respond and the reluctance of leadership to identify, encourage and instruct those potentially called-out ones.

Sustaining Workers

Prayer for identifying and commissioning workers is only the beginning of the process. It becomes even more important once workers have arrived among the peoples to whom they have been called. The church's most famous missionary, the Apostle Paul, reminded churches that they were co-workers with him in the missionary enterprise. As such they had a responsibility to continue supporting the work by praying that:

- God would provide opportunities for him to share the Gospel (Colossians 4:2-4).
- Their missionary outreach would continue (1 Thessalonians 5:25).
- The message would be well received (2 Thessalonians 3:1).
- Those of evil intent would be overcome (2 Thessalonians 3:2).

J.O. Fraser (1886-1938) was a missionary to the Lisu people in the mountainous regions of Yunan province in Southwest China. From 1910 till his death in 1938, he gave 28 years of his life to reaching these people. For the first six years his best efforts went unrewarded. Discouraged, he considered resigning his commission. However, before doing so he recruited vital intercessory prayer support back in the UK. That resulted in a spiritual breakthrough. In the period 1916-1918, 600 Lisu came to faith. A multiplying movement was birthed that not even the Communist conquest of China could suppress. By 1950 the number of believers had increased to 14,800. By 1995, 100,000 Lisu, representing approximately 95% of inhabitants in the Nujiang Lisu Autonomous Prefecture in Yunan Province, identified as Christian.

Earlier Fraser concluded, "I used to think that prayer should have the first place and teaching the second. I now feel it would be truer to give prayer the first, second and third places and teaching the fourth."[116]

Prayer had changed the whole work environment and

To pray is to change.

Prayer is the central

avenue God uses

to transform us.

---

116 J.O. Fraser, *The Prayer of Faith*. Sevenoaks, UK, Overseas Missionary Fellowship, 1958, 25.

Fraser himself. Sixty years later Richard Foster would write, "To pray is to change. Prayer is the central avenue God uses to transform us."[117]

Prayer Priorities

In praying for missions and missionaries, there are three areas that need constant attention. The **first** of these is for their **protection**. To venture into uncharted, previously spiritually uncontested territory without adequate prayer cover, is a dangerous folly. Satan does not withdraw and release his captives simply because a missionary appears on the scene. Without adequate prayer covering, disaster may be the result. But with it, Satan's attacks are defeated.

In 1960 the Mau Mau liberation movement spread terror throughout Kenya. At that time, missionaries Matt and Lora Higgens were aware of the danger involved in driving through Mau Mau controlled territory. Colleagues and others had already been murdered for using the road they needed to travel.

After dark, 27 kms (17 miles) from Nairobi, their otherwise reliable Land Rover broke down. Repair was not possible in the dark. All that Matt and Lora could do was to pray Psalm 4:8, "I will lie down and sleep in peace, for You alone, O Lord, make me dwell in safety."

The next morning after they awoke, Matt repaired the vehicle and they continued their journey to arrive safely in Nairobi. The next week a national pastor gave them a report of what he had learned about their incident. While the missionaries slept, three of the dreaded Mau Mau had crept up to the vehicle intending to kill them. But when they discovered that 16 men had already surrounded the vehicle and were standing guard, fearfully they fled the scene.

---

117   Richard J. Foster, *Celebration of Discipline*. New York, Harper and Row, 1978, 30.

Matt and Lora were thrilled but puzzled as to what it all meant. Only when they returned home to America was the mystery solved. There, a friend asked if they had recently been in a dangerous situation. They affirmed they had been and confirmed it had been on March 23. Excitedly the friend reported, that on precisely that date, he had felt so burdened for their safety, he called together other men of the church for an emergency prayer meeting. The number of men praying at that meeting was sixteen. In answer to their intercession, God positioned the same number of angels to protect His servants.[118]

If we fail to pray consistently for the protection of those whom we commission, there may be no need to pray for other issues. For a variety of reasons, the workers may have been neutralized or removed from the field.

The **second** area upon which prayer needs to be focused, is that those among whom the missionary labors, will see that the living **God answers prayers**.

As hundreds of Zulus trudged across the parched valleys and scorched earth of drought-stricken South Africa toward the village of Amatikulu, Salvation Army Officer, Captain Allister Smith, prayed fervently for rain. He was encouraged to see at least one Zulu had sufficient faith to bring an umbrella, in the hope that the foreigner's God might grant their plea for rain.

Captain Smith stood before the vast crowd, raised his voice and taught a simple prayer for rain in the Zulu language. With that, Smith and the handful of converts who were present, continued to pray fervently. Gradually the crowd joined in with a ripple of desperation. For three hours the white-hot sun beat down upon them as the crowd prayed on. Suddenly, from far away in the east, a low rumble was heard. Angry black clouds

---

118   Bill Bright, *Mau Mau Uprising*. Daily Inspirations, July 8, 2021. https://www. crosswalk.com/devotionals/insights-from-bill-bright/mau-mau-uprising-july-8.html (viewed May 13, 2022).

surged in from over the Indian Ocean, impatiently tumbling over one another. Lightening cracked and ripped into the ground nearby the trembling crowd. Dollops of rain spilled over from the roiling clouds now overhead, as they raced ahead like a numberless herd of stampeding wildebeest. The blackened clouds split open. The prayer meeting was washed out. Returning home was difficult for many trying to cross flooded raging streams.

As a result of this, Chief Tshingwayo, his witch doctors and all who belonged to his kraal, accepted the invitation to follow Jesus. The tribe would do likewise. The first Zulu school would be built to teach numeracy and literacy. Modern agricultural methods would be introduced along with basic building techniques. The role of women changed. No longer were they treated as beasts of burden. Trained animals would assume that role.

All of this and much more happened because Captain Allister Smith and his Scottish team believed in, practiced and experienced "the power of prevailing prayer."[119]

In India, Susanta Patra was sharing the gospel with 45 mostly professional Hindus in the city of Kolkata. Unexpectedly, a woman suffering with terminal cancer was presented to him. Then came the request. "Will you pray for her to show that your God is more powerful than the gods of Hinduism?"

Susanta was inexperienced in such matters. He felt overwhelmed. Nevertheless, he prayed. Then he fled home on his motorcycle. Thinking that nothing would have happened in response to his prayer, he was too embarrassed to return to the group at the customary time the next week. When he next attended, he was amazed to discover that the woman was completely healed and that the 45 enquirers had come to

---

119   Trevor Yaxley, *William and Catherine: The Life and Legacy of the Booths*. Ada, MI, Bethany House, 91.

faith in Jesus. Within a short time, a dozen new churches were commenced in that Bengali community.[120]

From childhood Omar went to the mosque to pray and religiously follow all the prescriptions of Islamic worship. But he often cried, "Allah, I would like to know you. Talk to me." When he shared his desire with another person, he received some challenging advice. It was that he should go to his room, kneel and call out to God in the respective names of Buddha, someone known to Hindus, Muhammad and Jesus. He was to make known his deep desire for a relationship with his creator and then see who see might answer.

He followed the advice. But from the first three there came no answer. Finally, he prayed in the name of Jesus. He later reported that when he prayed in the name of Jesus, '… it was as if someone walked into the room. All my hair stood on end. From my head to my feet, I felt as if someone was touching me. I heard a voice saying, "Omar, I am Jesus your Lord. I love you. Do you want to know more?"

"No, my Lord. I trust You. From now on, you are my Lord. Today You have answered me.'"[121]

The **third** area for focused prayer for cross-cultural workers, is for their courage to **prevail in spiritual power encounters**. As it was in the ministry of Jesus and in the Acts of the Apostles, power encounters are a frequent outcome, in daring to challenge Satan's hold over his captives and territory. Still today, most new churches in developing countries are formed from often explosive encounters of this kind. As Paul wrote, "Our gospel came to you not simply with words but also with power" (1 Thessalonians 1:5).

---

120 Ted Olsen, *Miracles show readiness for "Table 71" in India*. Dawn Report, Issue No. 47, June 2002, 1.

121 *'If only My People will Pray'*, Revival World report, September–October 2000, 18

In 2021, a small evangelistic team arrived in a non-Christian village in Togo. With permission they began to share the good news about Jesus. The people in this village had long been held enthralled by the power of Voodoo, which is common in Togo.

After a short while, local people asked the team leader to cease preaching. When asked for a reason for the request, they pointed to a large tree behind the speaker. Its leaves and branches were shaking as if agitated by strong wind. Except there was no wind. The locals attributed the phenomenon to their belief that their local demons inhabited that tree. Clearly, the tree's inhabitants were expressing their agitation and displeasure at what the preacher was saying.

The team leader, however, declined to desist. The effect upon the tree noticeably increased. With that some of the villagers hastened to call the local constabulary, who in turn upon their arrival, ordered the Christians to stop and leave the village. Reluctantly they agreed. As they did so, in a manner reminiscent of the events on Mount Carmel in 1 Kings 18, a massive bolt of lightning flashed from the heavens. It struck the tree, ripping it out of the ground and hurling onto its side, with its roots fully exposed to the air. That certainly grasped the attention of the local people. News travelled to the tribal chief. Upon his arrival, he commented on the power of the God of the Bible. He then wanted to know what they had to do to establish a church within his domain, so they could learn more of this God.

A sad but not unexpected outcome from this event was, that when the story was repeated in a developed country, even with photographic evidence to support the claims, the story was still questioned as to its authenticity. Fortunately, people in Togo do not entertain such doubts.

Failure to Pray

Missionaries on furlough often encounter well-meaning believers who greet them at the church door as they depart the meeting. With good intent, missionaries are reassured they will not be forgotten. They will be prayed for. But often there is no further contact.

The effects of that all-too-common occurrence are two-fold:

1. There will be insufficient laborers in the field to bring in the harvest of which Jesus spoke.

2. Those in the field, not being sustained through prayer and other support, will be more quickly neutralized and withdrawn.

Paul, in his letter to the Roman believers, addressed the first problem. He expressed it as follows:

"Everyone who calls upon the name of the Lord will be saved. How then can they call on the one they have not believed in? And how can they believe in the one of whom they have not heard? And how can they hear without someone preaching to them? And how can they preach unless they are sent?" (Romans 10:13-15).

Paul's logic leads inevitably to a brutally grotesque outcome.

If no one is sent, then no one preaches.
If no one preaches, no one can hear.
If no one hears, no one can believe.
If no one believes, no one can call upon the name of the Lord.
If no one calls upon the name of the Lord, no one can be saved.

What might that look like?

In November 1970, a severe storm swept up the Bay of Bengal. As the borders of the Bay narrowed, water was pushed higher and higher before the relentless force of the storm. Eventually, a giant tidal wave formed that crashed into the remote shores of what was then called East Pakistan. Today it is renamed Bangladesh.

A massive wall of water surged inland for many kilometers across the flat plain, sweeping aside everything in its path. It then returned to the ocean, sucking every movable object with it as it went. In the aftermath no living creature remained. Everything was flattened and destroyed. In the weeks that followed, the sun relentlessly beat down in the near total silence that shrouded the cracked bare muddied plain. The only movement that occasionally could be seen or heard, was the futile flapping of vultures' wings. In vain they tried to fly. They could not, because they had over-gorged on the rotting flesh of animals and humans.

It was later estimated that in that one night alone 500,000 people perished. As far as is known, not one of them had ever had a chance of hearing the good news of Jesus.

That event was followed four months later by the commencement of the War of Independence. With India's help, that resulted in the birth of Bangladesh in November 1971. In that 10-month conflict, another 3,000,000 people were killed. Only a handful of them would have had any opportunity of considering the claims of Christ.

Meanwhile back in the commissioning countries, Christians continue to have a numbing variety of choice, as to what Christian message they may listen to daily via radio, TV or their local church. This raises a critical question—why should anyone hear the message twice, before everyone has heard it once?

This brings us to the second situation, the sustainability of workers.

William Carey agreed to venture into the uncharted territory of Hindu Bengal in India, provided his colleagues back home agreed "to hold the ropes." In that way, he was asking them to commit to pray for him and to support the work financially.

With a similar assurance, a young missionary couple travelled to the place of their appointment. But two years later the husband returned home alone. He was a broken man. Unnoticed, he slipped into a back seat of his church's mid-week prayer meeting. He listened attentively. At the end he stood and said, "I am your missionary whom you sent forth. My wife and child lie buried in Africa and I am sick with disease. I listened to your prayers to see if you kept your promise. It was in vain. You failed to hold the ropes!"

But what if we did persevere in prayer and "hold the ropes" for those who were commissioned to go?

A Case Study–Nepal

A mission to Nepal was established in 1715 by Roman Catholic friars of the Capuchin order. They were all expelled by 1769. For Christian missions, Nepal remained a closed Hindu kingdom. During the early 20th century, to minister to visiting Nepalese, missionary outposts were established along Nepal's border with India.

In the city of Melbourne, Australia, in those years every Friday night believers gathered to pray for Nepal to open. That finally happened after the revolution against the ruling Rana dynasty in 1951. Missionaries were permitted to enter under strict conditions. Proselytization and conversion were prohibited and, to this day, are still legally banned.

Nevertheless, despite persecution or because of it, the number of Christians in Nepal is estimated to be between 1–3 million believers.

This has resulted in one academic study concluding that the Nepali church in recent years has been the fastest growing in the world.[122] How could this be? One factor from one of many such examples provides an answer.

Andrew Smith[123] and his wife, supported by a team of intercessors, arrived in Nepal in March 1969. Trekking across the Himalayas, in November 1969, they found the Magar people in the village of Deurali. In 1971 they moved across the mountains to another Magar village of Thankot. The Magar people numbered approximately 300,000. They asked their intercessors to pray for the Magars wherever they might be found. The nearest church was a three-day trek through the mountains in distant Pokhara.

God's people did pray.

After 4 years of discouragements, an old one-legged soldier came to be with them. In July 1973, Baju confessed his many sins, was baptized and commenced his adventure with Jesus.

God's people continued to pray.

In 1974, Scripture translation began. Baju frequently trekked across the mountains sharing his faith, supported by his bamboo crutches. Persecution was severe. Therefore, very few responded to the message. In 1976 the Smith family was expelled from Nepal.

But God's people continued to pray.

Many hundreds of kilometers distant in East Nepal, Sikkim and Bhutan, there lived scattered communities of Magar who had migrated there about two centuries earlier. In 1984, a 15-year-old Magar boy, who for three years had been dangerously ill,

---

122 Scott Hamilton, *Christianity in its Global Context, 1970–2020: Society, Religion and Mission*. South Hamilton, MA, Center for the Study for Global Christianity, 38. (Viewed January 27, 2019).

123 Names and locations relating to Nepal have been changed by request, to avoid further persecution.

attended a Christian meeting. He was miraculously healed. But when he returned home, his Hindu father was so incensed, he paid thugs to kill his son. Twice he was ambushed, being stabbed and beaten with iron rods. He survived and today oversees 25 churches.

God's people continued to pray for the Magars.

In 1992 a young Magar teenager accepted Jesus. He was beaten, tortured and jailed. In March 1993, he found a place in a refugee camp in East Nepal. In 1994 he was jailed again for his witnessing. Later after his release in 2009, he was granted refugee status in the US where he now pastors a thriving church of Magars in Austin, Texas.

Another Magar believer in Bhutan was given poisoned milk which was "accidently" spilt. The cats drank it and died. As a refugee, he pastors a Magar church of over 300 people in Atlanta, Georgia.

And still God's people continued to pray for the Magars.

In fact, in October 1993, at least 4,300 intercessors agreed to focus prayer on Nepal. 180 of them even travelled to Nepal to pray on site.[124]

Meanwhile back in Deurali, which Andrew Smith and members of his family had continued to visit for months each year, a fine new church building was completed in October 2021. Despite more persecution, as a result of many deliverances from demonic infestations, miraculous healings, faithful preaching, with prayer and fasting, churches of new believers are today scattered across the mountainous homeland of the Magars.

Away to the East where other Magars had migrated and which was the scene of severe persecutions, about 2,000 Magars accepted Jesus at the turn of this century. By 2022,

---

124   Luis Bush, *Reaching every people group in Nepal for Christ,* MARC Newsletter, Number 96-1, March 1996, 6.

their number had increased to approximately 15,000.[125]

It continues to happen, as God's people persist in prayer.

If we are to complete the task of bringing in the harvest to which Jesus referred, prayer must become our top priority. As Tom Wells explains: "Prayer is our first work in the harvest... The reason is... the harvest has a "Lord". He oversees the harvest. (He) supplies workers... Our first business is to pray to our God."[126]

> To complete the task of bringing in the harvest prayer must become our top priority.

125   Andrew Smith, Personal Correspondence 2016-2022.
126   Tom Wells, *A Vision for Missions*. Carlisle, Pennsylvania, Banner of Truth, 1985, 138.

Chapter 10
TOUGH TRAINING

*Fasting is the secret key that unlocks heaven's
door and slams shut the gates of hell.*

Jentezen Franklin (1962–)

In the city of Dhaka, Bangladesh, Calvin Olsen saw a cow on the ground about to have its throat cut with a large sharp knife. It was to serve as a sacrifice in front of a mosque. He stopped his car, took a few photos and drove home. That night the Holy Spirit challenged him to act less as a tourist and to be more diligent in fulfilling his calling as a bearer of the Good News of Jesus. He was directed to commence praying and fasting and then to return to where he had photographed the animal sacrifice. He was further instructed to tell those present, of the greater sacrifice that Jesus had provided already, by His willingly dying on the cross on behalf of us all.

Somewhat chastened, in the streaming pre-monsoon heat of the next day, he set off to return to the scene of his previous day's photography. Over his shoulder, he carried a bag of Gospel tracts to give to whomever he met. He also carried some small copies of various gospels that he would offer for sale at cost of production. People value more something they pay for, than that given free of charge. Having sold his stock and distributed all the other literature, he returned home well pleased with his morning's effort. He also felt good about his obedience to the Spirit's prompting. The assignment was completed. Or so he thought.

Mission Incomplete

That night as he prayed over the day's events, again the Spirit impressed upon him to continue his fast and to return to the vicinity of the mosque in the bazaar, to repeat what he had done that day. Obediently he followed instructions.

Night two the instructions were repeated. "Continue praying and fasting. Go to the same location to hand out tracts. Sell whatever copies of the Gospels you can." Night after night after night, instructions were given and obeyed the next day.

Eventually local Muslims were stirred to oppose the man, his message and his mission. He was warned that should he continue, there would be consequences for him and his property. To reinforce their intention, a mob dragged him through the bazaar, doused him in dye, kicked him into a dirty ditch and stoned him where he lay. Twice a zealot tried to stab him with a knife, which had he succeeded, would have resulted in a quick but painful death. Fortunately, he was restrained by others in the crowd.

Two well-muscled appropriately experienced trouble-shooters were appointed to keep watch, should this messenger ever dare to return. In the event of that happening, it had been made perfectly clear, the Lord's servant would not leave the area in a rickshaw next time. He would require an ambulance to transport his body to the nearest morgue.

Confronted with such obvious danger, the missionary continued to pray and fast to discern whatever might be the Spirit's next instruction.

On day forty of his fast the Word came to him. It was that he must return to the site from which he had been so painfully ejected. Mindful of the warning never to return, reluctantly he bade farewell to his wife. They both realized that because of the likelihood of his being killed, this might be their last farewell.

The Lord's Intervention

Slowly he returned to the site of the earlier conflict. No sooner had he arrived when news of his return went out. Quickly the muscular minders were on the scene. A hostile mob soon gathered anticipating a spectacle of what they thought was about to happen. Agitators whipped up the crowd with calls to kill the infidel. However, just as the crowd's blood lust for violence was about to be satisfied, two tall strangers speared through the crowd. In one fluid movement, they grasped the missionary and ushered him swiftly down a lane to where a pedal rickshaw was waiting. Placing their rescued cargo in the rickshaw, they spoke to him for the first and last time.

"It is enough for now. You don't need to come back here again."

The rickshaw moved off. The two tall strangers were never seen again. That night the Lord addressed His servant once more as he knelt in prayer. "Now you know how much I love and care for Muslims. It is not My will that any of them should perish without first hearing the message of salvation that I have prepared for those who will receive it."

Although this missionary and his message were reviled and rejected by the mob, through prayer and fasting he had attracted the favor of God. It could only have been God who touched the heart of the then president of Bangladesh, Chief Justice Abu Sayeed Chowdhury (1921–1987). He was so impressed by the life of this dedicated foreigner, that he rented one of his own homes to

> When persistent prayer is combined with fasting, powerful spiritual forces are unleashed to achieve what God wants.

him at a very reasonable price. Then he sold a piece of his own prime land to the missionary to build what became at that time, the largest Protestant church in the nation. All the finance and specialized trade persons were provided repeatedly at exactly the right time, as Calvin continued to fast and pray.

When persistent prayer is combined with fasting, powerful spiritual forces are unleashed to achieve what God wants, even though the world declares such to be impossible.

Fasting–Today?

Today however, at least in the Western church, fasting is hardly a widespread spiritual discipline. More attention is diverted to dieting to overcome the common outcome from overeating–obesity.

Fasting has become a political device in many countries. It is used to pressure governments to grant concessions they would not otherwise make. It is also used as a means of fundraising by some well-known charities.

As Islam has spread in the West, the practice of fasting during the daylight hours of the Muslim month of Ramadan, has become widely recognized. But in the church, it is hardly ever mentioned, let alone practiced. Therefore, it may come as a surprise to learn how much the Bible has to say on this subject and how strongly it is commended.

In History

Within the Biblical context, fasting means "voluntarily to abstain from eating food for spiritual purposes."[127] Derek Prince believed "fasting is the revealed will of God for every professing Christian."[128] It is often proclaimed in the Old Testament,

---

127 Allan Webb, *Fast and Pray*. East Asia's Millions, Vol.105, 1997 No.3, 2.

128 Derek Prince, *Secrets of a Prayer Warrior*. Grand Rapids, Michigan, Chosen, 2009, 167.

presented by Jesus in the Gospels, promoted by the Apostles and practiced in the early church of the New Testament era.

In more recent history, those whom God used mightily to found new movements that gave rise to today's denominations and mission agencies, were often people who not only prayed persistently, but they also fasted frequently.

Martin Luther (1483-1546) in Germany, John Calvin (1509-1564) in Switzerland, John Knox (1514-1572) in Scotland, John Wesley (1703-1791) in England, Charles Finney (1792-1875) in America, Hudson Taylor (1832-1905) in China, Mother Theresa (1910-1997) in India, David Yonggi Cho (1936-2021) in Korea—all these were used to effect change within nations and influence others for generations to come—by prayer and fasting.

In the Bible

Ezra was handed a difficult assignment. He was responsible for escorting a large party of men, women and children all the way from where they had been in exile in Babylon, back to the rubble of what remained of the ruins of Jerusalem. Additionally, he had to carry back the very valuable sacred vessels to be used again whenever the Temple was reconstructed.

Leading a large, unarmed party of people, who were also carrying an extremely valuable cargo, through many hundreds of kilometers of brigand infested territory, presented incalculable dangers. The obvious precaution to take, was to at least deploy an armed security detail. It would need to be of a size that would cause would-be raiding parties to think twice before launching an attack. But Ezra felt that hiring a protective security detail was something he could not do. This was because in presenting his case to the king, he had confidently declared that "the good hand of our God is on everyone who looks to Him, but His great anger is against all who forsake Him" (Ezra 8:22).

Having so impressed the king by the boldness of his faith in God, Ezra would have heaped shame upon his own head, by further requesting a detachment of troops to provide protection. This would have indicated that the God of whom he had boasted, was now inadequate to provide the needed protection. He'd painted himself into a corner, within a room of his own construction! If he was to avoid bringing everything crashing down around him, what could he do?

The answer? "...we fasted and petitioned our God about this, and He answered our prayer" (Ezra 8:23).

The result? "The hand of our God was on us, and He protected us from enemies and bandits along the way" (Ezra 8:31). From the Ahava Canal in Babylon, right around the Fertile Crescent to Jerusalem, not a single threat occurred to disrupt the successful outcome of this operation. The natural odds against such would have been incalculably high.

If Ezra's valiant leadership of the returning party with their sacred treasure was challenging, even more so was what followed. To repopulate Jerusalem with descendants of its original inhabitants was one thing. To rebuild the city from the rubble of its ruined state, against all local opposition, was a challenge of a completely different order.

The person of the Lord's choice for this task was **Nehemiah**. He was a cupbearer in the service of King Artaxerxes in Susa. When he heard of the distressed state of the exiles who had returned to Jerusalem and the neglected condition of their habitation, he was greatly disturbed. But what could he do? He was only a very low ranking official in the king's court. One misplaced word on his part could see him discharged, exiled or even executed.

Nehemiah's response? "For some days I mourned and fasted and prayed before the God of heaven" (Nehemiah 1:4).

Everything that followed, the overcoming of many threats, difficulties and obstructions, right up to the eventual success of rebuilding the walls of Jerusalem, flowed from Nehemiah's time of prayer and fasting.

If these events seem amazing to our faith that has been impaired by our twenty-first century outlook that places a high priority on science, how do we evaluate the miraculous saving of an entire nation through little more than prayer and fasting? Adolf Hitler's Holocaust policy threatened approximately one-third of international Jewry in the 1940s. But in the 5th century BC, the entire population of Jews was under sentence of death. There had never been a more serious threat to God's chosen people up to that time. Nor has there been a crisis of greater magnitude since then.

As the result of a carefully crafted conspiracy, an edict in the name of King Xerxes had gone out across the empire from the city of Susa. A court official, "Haman, son of Hammedatha the Agagite, the enemy of the Jews" (Esther 3:10), had manipulated circumstances to persuade Xerxes to sign the death warrant of all Jews within his domain. None would be exempted. The date was set. The king's seal meant it was written into "the laws of Persia and Media, which (could not) be repealed" (Esther 1:19). That principle resulted in the dethronement of Queen Vashti. Now it would be applied to the killing of all Jews in every province (Esther 3:8–15).

How could this royally sanctioned genocide be averted?

The answer lay with an otherwise unknown Jewish girl, **Hadassah**, also known as **Esther**. She had been suddenly elevated to replace the dethroned Vashti. Queen Esther had been informed of the plot by her uncle Mordecai. Only she could have any hope of influencing a different outcome.

Esther well knew, that to dare to enter the king's presence without prior permission, could be at the cost of her life. But as Uncle Mordecai had said, "...who knows but that you have come to royal position for such a time as this?" (Esther 4:14). Given her knowledge of the long history of her people, Esther was fully aware that it was ultimately God who controlled and directed all the seemingly insignificant coincidences of life. For the possibility of saving her people, she willingly put her own life on the line. She agreed to appear unannounced before the king. "And if I perish, I perish" (Esther 4:16). But there was a proviso to her seeming recklessness.

To Mordecai she sent one vital instruction, "Go, gather together all the Jews who are in Susa, and fast for me. Do not eat or drink for three days, night or day. I and my maids will fast as you do. When this is done, I will go to the king, even though it is against the law" (Esther 4:16). Every Jew knew that fasting for special purposes was automatically within the context of extended prayer.

By prioritizing prayer and fasting, Esther did what Old Testament leaders did. From a human perspective she understood the near impossibility of the task before her. Appreciating the spiritual implications involved, she moved the conflict from the realm of the natural to that of the spiritual.

Satan's emissary, Haman, in setting the date of execution, had engaged those with expertise in the dark arts—the court magicians. They had cast lots to determine the most auspicious day for the deadly deed (Esther 3:7). Haman had waited almost a full year in sweet anticipation of this outcome. With Esther's insertion of prayer and fasting, the spiritual battle lines were drawn.

In an extraordinary sequence of events, the fortunes of Haman's overreach were unraveled. The genocidal death threat was averted at the last moment. There was an execution, not of the Jews, but of Haman. God's people were saved through God's response to their implementation of prayer and fasting.

That miraculous event is still remembered in the annual festival of Purim by all Jews till this day. It is celebrated according to the Jewish calendar on Adar 14–15.

Throughout the Old Testament the precedent and practice of fasting was cemented into Israelite religious consciousness.

The great lawgiver Moses fasted for 40 days on Mount Horeb (Exodus 34:28).

Joshua and the elders of Israel fasted after their army's defeat at Ai (Joshua 7:6).

The 11 tribes of Israel fasted at Gibeah (Judges 20:26).

The Israelites hard pressed by the Philistines fasted at Mizpah (1 Samuel 7:6).

King David fasted to try to save the life of his child conceived as the result of an adulterous affair with Bathsheba (2 Samuel 12:16).

Joel declared a fast to counter the effects of a drought and a devastating locust plague (Joel 1:14; 2:12,15).

The practice was so common, that by the time of Jesus, there was hardly need for additional teaching by Him. However, He did fast for 40 days before commencing His public ministry (Matthew 4:2). He clearly indicated His disciples would fast after His departure (Luke 5:33). And to them He did not say "If you fast" but "**When** you fast" (Matthew 6:16–18).

The Early Church

The example of fasting was not lost on the early church. While they were ministering to the Lord and fasting, the first cross-cultural workers were identified and commissioned (Acts 13:1–3). In each new church elders were appointed with prayer and fasting (Acts 14:23).

The Apostle Paul said he often went without food (2 Corinthians 11:27) and was hungry (1 Corinthians 4:11). These occasions may not have been of his choosing. But like all the other hardships that he endured, he embraced these experiences as an outcome of the ministry to which he had been called. He was determined not to gratify desires which come through his natural self (Galatians 5:16–17). Just as every serious athlete trains to win a prize, so Paul also trained. He disciplined his body (1 Corinthians 9:24–27).

Jesus said that if we want to follow Him then we must deny ourselves (Matthew 16:24).

Self-discipline

One of the ways to train, to discipline our bodies, to exercise self-control, is in the commonest area of our appetites—our desire for food. Our stomachs will protest. But by fasting we respond by signaling to that often greedy bodily organ, "You are not in charge. You do not dictate. You will neither master nor oversee my life."

In the context of physical versus spiritual appetites for supremacy, the pandemic of obesity in the West, clearly demonstrates where the priority of our habits has led us –and shortened our lives as well.

Apart from the obvious reason of self-denial being a means of disciplining our physical appetites, why else should we fast?

Benefits of Fasting

Many testify that fasting helps to clear the clutter in our minds. It accumulates through the barrage transmitted through our physical senses. The noise of the world that constantly clamors for our attention, serves to distract us from setting ourselves to hear from God. Just as excessively noisy machinery can cause industrial deafness, so the shouting of the multiple voices of the world, demanding our attention, sets us up for spiritual deafness.

God does not compete with every other noise to get our attention. If we would hear Him, He advises, "Be still and know that I am God" (Psalm 46:10). It then follows that we might know that "The Lord Almighty is with us" (Psalm 46:11). Fasting sets the scene for this possibility.

Bill Bright (1921–2003) was used by God to commence an international ministry originally known as *Campus Crusade for Christ*. In 2011 its name was changed to *Cru*. He believed passionately in prayer and fasting. He wrote extensively on these subjects. In 1995 he published *The Coming Revival*.[129] Based upon his personal experience, his study of Scripture, the early church Fathers and Church leadership in history up to the present time, Bright saw the need for fasting:

- To bring revelation by the Holy Spirit of our true spiritual condition. This should cause us to repent and change our ways.
- As a means of personal revival as the Holy Spirit has greater access to us.
- To understand and apply the Word of God better in our lives.
- To transform prayer into a more vital personal experience.
- To strengthen spiritual determination.
- To restore our love for and intimacy with the Lord to what it is meant to be.

When

Obviously, the practice of fasting cannot be a continuous state. That would lead to the certainty of death. So, when may it be appropriate to fast?

---

129   Bill Bright, *The Coming Revival*. Campus Crusade for Christ, Orlando, Florida, 1995.

Pastor Allan Webb was used by God to grow the largest church in the nation for his denomination, the Australian Churches of Christ. In his time as Senior Pastor, the church commissioned countless missionaries whom they also supported financially. After 25 years he next became the national leader of the Overseas Missionary Fellowship (OMF). Based upon his careful study of the Bible and from his vast experience, he concluded there is a need to fast prior to:

> **Wesley urged all his followers to fast weekly as a matter of healthy spiritual discipline.**

- Times of great personal temptation.
- Making momentous decisions.
- Penetrating previously unreached areas with the Gospel.
- Encountering times of extraordinary difficulty.[130]

National Implications

John Wesley was used by God to reignite the spiritual flame of renewal within England. According to some historians, this avoided the bloody carnage which was happening across the English Channel in the French Revolution. Wesley urged all his followers to fast weekly as a matter of healthy spiritual discipline. He would not consider any person to become a candidate for ordination for ministry, unless they vowed to fast each Wednesday and Friday.

Around the same time, having won its War of Independence from Britain in 1777, the American Congress requested President George Washington to declare a day of national thanksgiving to Almighty God, for its military victory, for the new government and the Constitution that when adopted,

---

130 Webb, 4.

would create the United States of America. Washington issued the Proclamation on October 3, 1789. He designated Thursday, November 26, 1789, as a day of National Thanksgiving.

The Proclamation urged the citizens of the new nation, not just to thank God for their military victories that won their independence and the subsequent development of their unique form of government. It also urged all to pray for forgiveness for national and other sins, to be loving toward one another and to remain humble. Without this they could never hope to be a "happy nation".[131]

Within a century, many people forgot that God had helped them to obtain freedoms upon which their prosperity was dependent. Instead, while they enjoyed their unfettered freedom, they allowed the slavery of others to flourish in their midst. The result was, "a recognition of the hand of God in (a) terrible visitation" that afflicted the nation with division and civil war.[132] Consequently, A Day of Prayer and Fasting was declared for August 12, 1861. However, the war continued.

In 1863, "The senate of the United States, devoutly recognizing the supreme authority and just government of Almighty God in all the affairs of men and of nations," requested President Abraham Lincoln to declare another Day of National Humiliation, Fasting and Prayer.

In Proclamation 97, Lincoln urged all to confess their sins, to humble themselves and to repent. He acknowledged that,

> [They] had been the recipients of the choicest bounties of Heaven… Of peace and prosperity … wealth and power. But we have forgotten God… We have vainly imagined,

---

131   Eddie L. Hyatt, *1726: The Year that Defined America.* Grapevine, Texas, Hyatt International Ministries, 2019, 120.

132   Abraham Lincoln, *Proclamation 85–Proclaiming a Day of National Humiliation, Prayer and Fasting, August 2, 1861.* https://www.presidency.ucsb.edu/documents/proclamation-85-proclaiming-day-national-humiliation-prayer-and-fasting (Viewed June 17, 2022).

in the deceitfulness of our hearts, that all these blessings [have come] by some superior wisdom and virtue of our own. Intoxicated with our own unbroken success, we have become... too proud to pray to the God who made us.

In the light of this, the President called for Thursday April 30, 1863, to be set aside for "national humiliation, fasting and prayer."[133]

Following this National Day of Prayer and Fasting, the direction of the war shifted in favor of the northern union. The Battle of Gettysburg, in Pennsylvania on July 1-3, 1863, was the beginning of the end. "National repentance, prayer (and fasting) changed the course of history." [134]

Prayer and fasting were not only at the behest of the Senate or the President. It was a familiar event at State and local levels in the United States.

Locust plagues were well known to Minnesota farmers. Their crops had been destroyed by the voraciously hungry insects in the summer of 1876. Now in the spring of 1877 they waited and watched to see whether such pestilence would strike yet again. If it did, the farming future of thousands of families would be wiped out – permanently.

Acutely aware of the impending disaster, Governor J.S. Pillsbury proclaimed that April 26 would be a day of prayer and fasting to plead with God, to save them from calamity. The Governor urged that every single person should unite and participate toward this end.

---

133   Abraham Lincoln, *Proclamation 97–Appointing a Day of National Humiliation, Fasting and Prayer, March 30.1863*. https://www.presidency.ucsb.edu/documents/proclamation-97-appointing-day-national-humiliation-fasting-and-prayer (Viewed June 17, 2022).

134   Eddie Hyatt, *A Message for America from Her Two Greatest Presidents*. https://www.charismanews.com/culture/89296-a-message-for-america-from-her-two-greatest-presidents. May 27,2022.

Across the state people responded to their Governor's call. In gatherings large and small Minnesotans assembled to fast and pray.

The very next day as the sun soared in a cloudless sky, with temperatures also rising, the people noticed to their dismay that the dreaded insects started to stir in the warmed soil.

For three more days the uninterrupted unseasonal heat caused a vast army of locusts to hatch. It was of such plague proportions as to threaten the entire North-West farm sector. Then, as the sun departed at the end of that fourth day, with the locusts all hatched and ready to move, a sudden climatic change flicked a blanket of frost across the entire area where the locusts waited for dawn and take-off. Most were killed right where they crouched. Come summer, instead of scorched stubbled dirt, as far as the eye could see, the wheat crop waved in golden glory. In the history of Minnesota, April 26, 1877, is recorded as the day when God wonderfully responded to the prayers and fasting of his people.

If America's rise to world prominence in the twentieth century, could be explained partly by its spiritual foundations in the nineteenth century, what might be its predictable future in the twenty-first century? From Old Testament history one thing is certain. Whenever the nation of Israel walked away from God's laws and standards, disaster followed shortly thereafter, until leaders led the nation in repentance back to God.

> **Fasting is something between us and God... lest it become little more than legalistic habits.**

In 2019, the Democratic National Committee unanimously affirmed atheism and declared that neither Christianity nor any religion is necessary for morality or patriotism.[135] Whither America?

Why

Some of the above indicates when it is appropriate to fast. Even so, we still need to ask ourselves why we are doing this. It's easy and spiritually disingenuous to engage in self-denial practices just to impress others. In giving to the needy, praying and fasting, Jesus specifically warned against doing this in ways that would attract the attention of others.

Those who look for the approval of others by such means, will certainly attract no reward in heaven (Matthew 6:1). In fact, Jesus taught that His followers should deliberately go further in the opposite direction. "When you fast, do not look somber as the hypocrites do… .to show men they are fasting… But when you fast put oil on your head and wash your face so that it will not be obvious to men that you are fasting" (Matthew 6:16-18).

In other words, act normally. Be cheery. Fasting is something between us and God.

Jesus "was led by the Spirit" (Matthew 4:1) to commence his 40 days of fasting. We need to be similarly sure that we also are truly led into similar spiritual exercises, lest they become little more than legalistic habits, serving no useful purpose other than temporary weight loss.

Our objective is to increase intimacy with our Heavenly Father. By fasting, we might hear from Him more clearly in an atmosphere of lessened distraction.

The early church gave itself over to ministering to the Lord in worship as they prayed and fasted. It was then they were able to hear clearly the Holy Spirit's instructions regarding the call to Barnabas and Saul. This was a momentous decision,

---

135 Hyatt, ibid

that as history would show, had world changing implications (Acts 13:1-3). If we claim to be a "New Testament" people, we ought to follow their example and expect similar outcomes. In worship, we minister to the Lord who "is the same yesterday and today and forever" (Hebrews 13:8).

Precautionary Advice

Irrespective of any of the above, if one has any abnormal medical conditions, before commencing any fast, it is appropriate firstly to consult a medical doctor for advice. When beginning a fast, be aware that in the first three days, headaches and hunger may be normal. Headaches commonly occur because most people daily imbibe caffeine through drinking tea, coffee or cola soft drinks. When caffeine is suddenly denied, the body's response during "withdrawal" is a headache.

When completing a fast caution is required. Small helpings of food taken more regularly, gradually restore all bodily systems without discomfort.

While in general the Biblical form of fasting is abstinence from food, the same does not apply to fluid intake. Jesus did go without food for 40 days. Others have done likewise. It would seem to be a physical possibility. However, it is impossible to survive an equally long period totally without fluid intake. To avoid permanent physical impairment and death, it is necessary to maintain a normal intake of water to keep the body hydrated.

True and False Fasting

Isaiah 58 provides a comprehensive guide to the spiritual and physical benefits of fasting. It shines a light into the darkness of insincere fasting and in that event, what happens from God's perspective. It also provides great hope of what we may expect when fasting is undertaken in accordance with God's standards.

At the time of Isaiah, everything appeared proper—externally. The people seemed eager to seek God, for God to "draw near", to intervene in their affairs for their benefit (vs.1–3). Therefore, according to their ancient well-known traditions, they seemed to humble themselves, even covering themselves in sackcloth and ashes (v.5). And yes, they were also fasting (v.3). From the outside all looked good. But no matter how good our external appearance seems to be, God who reads our hearts, is far more interested in our internal condition. That gives rise to our motives.

Motives

From the times of Samuel and King David these matters were well known. "The Lord does not look at the things man looks at. Man looks at the outward appearance, but the Lord looks at the heart" (1 Samuel 16:7).

"… The Lord searches every heart and understands every motive behind the thoughts. If you seek Him, He will be found by you, but if you forsake Him, He will reject you forever" (1 Chronicles 28:9).

Nevertheless, this seemed to have been forgotten. The people of Isaiah's day were fasting and humbling themselves. But nothing of consequence was happening to alleviate whatever adverse condition had befallen them. Why so? The Lord made it very clear through His prophet Isaiah.

While they were fasting, they continued to bicker, quarrel, fight and cause all manner of strife among themselves. They were also engaging in malicious gossip and exploiting disadvantaged workers in their midst (vs. 3–4).

To attract God's favor, a radical change of heart and behavior was necessary. His requirements included justice and fair dealing, generosity toward any in need, shelter and clothing for any lacking in those things.

Unless they changed to fulfil God's preconditions, they could fast and pray all they liked. But it would be to no effect. Their straightened condition would continue.

However, should they choose to repent of their self-centered activities and behaviors, then God's blessings and rewards would be forthcoming. They would experience prosperity. Even their drought-stricken land would be revived by refreshing rains. The conditions would resemble the best of what it had been in their long history.

The words of their lawgiver Moses would have reminded them of all this. Through him, the Lord had succinctly declared:

> "And now, O Israel, what does the Lord your God ask of you but to fear the Lord your God, to walk in all His ways, to love Him, to serve the Lord your God with all your heart and with all your soul and to observe the Lord's commands and decrees that I am giving you today **for your own good**" (Deuteronomy 10:12).

What could be clearer and more comprehensive than that? Whether or not we understand the reasoning behind God's "laws", they are ultimately for our own benefit. The neglect of God's directives, thinking we can do better by enacting our own legislation in our day, underscores the reason we have so many intractable problems in our societies today. Neither affluence nor legislation can compensate or cure the spiritual malaise evident in our various jurisdictions.

That applies to nations and to God's people—the church. The foundation for any change for the better, always lies with God's people beginning to take seriously the matter of prayer and fasting. When they do, God's favor is seldom long in coming.

Wayman Rogers was somewhat disheartened with the lack of responsiveness to his ministry among his people. He did what many other pastors do in similar situations. He applied for a

> If we are ready and willing to surrender ourselves completely, we may even experience revival.

job with another church. In the process of so doing, the Lord interrupted him, just as He did when disheartened Jonah was avoiding carrying out the Lord's instructions in his day (Jonah 4). The Lord promised Pastor Rogers that if he returned to his original pastorate and enrolled others who would take prayer seriously, He would favor their requests. Having recruited sufficient people to pray in a 24/7 chain, the pastor and his people entreated the Lord to grow their number, among other requests. Against all previous trends the congregation grew from 200 to 2000. Then in addition to continuous prayer, the people decided they would also fast every Thursday. That's when the supernatural really broke through!

As Pastor Rogers reported:

> A woman with cancer was healed. God delivered people from demon possession. Many people were healed by the miraculous power of God. For four and a half months we had a revival where 10,000 people came each week to our church. They argued over who was going to get the front seats. People were saved and healed and 4600 people gave their hearts to God in that time. This was after the church had fasted and prayed for two years. The only problem we had was traffic jams...[136]

When we reset our priorities to seek God first (Matthew 6:33) and meet His conditions, His blessing in abundance will be poured out upon us. If we are ready and willing to surrender ourselves completely, we may even experience revival.

---

136 Wayman Rogers, *Fasting*. Church Growth, December 1988.

Chapter 11
A SAD SCENE

*Revival is the inrush of the Spirit into a body
that threatens to become a corpse.*

D.M. Panton (1870–1955)

The Call

In January 1998 in San Francisco, USA, a significant 36-page document was released. It had been drafted by a committee representing The Mission America Coalition, The National Revival Network and America's National Prayer Committee. In a covering letter explaining the reason for the document, the authors of *An Urgent Appeal*, noted the continuing quantitative and qualitative decline of the church in America. They further noted that the lifestyles of Christians and non-Christians in the nation were virtually indistinguishable. Consequently, Christ was not glorified as He deserved to be.

The full title of the document was: *An Urgent Appeal to Christian Leaders in America for Consensus and Collaboration of the Biblical Nature and Hope of Corporate Revival.*[137]

Christian luminaries of that era, denominational leaders, para-church leaders—Billy Graham, Bill Bright, Ron Sider and many others—signed in support of the document's stated aims. It was then released to the church nationwide. Readers were

---

137 *An Urgent Appeal to Christian Leaders in America for Consensus and Collaboration of the Biblical Nature and Hope of Corporate Revival.* https://static1.squarespace. com/static/6039a2aaa0caae5783b8b88b/t/608b57194cae1d36340603 cd/1619744540560/an_urgent_appeal.pdf. (Viewed June 29, 2022).

invited to sign a *Declaration of Intent* thereby committing themselves to at least pray for revival.

The preface of the document in part stated:

> In recognition of our absolute dependence on God; the moral and spiritual challenges facing our nation; our national need for repentance and divine intervention; our great hope for a general awakening to the lordship of Christ, the unity of His body and the sovereignty of His Kingdom; the unique opportunity that the dawn of a new millennium presents to us for offering the Gospel of Christ to everyone in our nation— We strongly urge all churches and all Christians of America to unite in seeking the face of God through prayer and fasting, persistently asking our Father to send revival to the church and spiritual awakening to our nation, so that Christ's great Commission might be fulfilled worldwide in our generation.

Another Call

There were many "calls" made to the churches as the new millennium approached—especially in America. One well-known "prophet", believing that the Y2K computer glitch would be the cause of multiple unthinkable disasters at the stroke of midnight 2000, encouraged the faithful to hoard food supplies and head for the hills. There, duly armed with appropriate firepower, they would be better equipped to beat off hungry hordes of unbelievers. Upon the eventual demise of the aforesaid unbelievers, the faithful would be able to safely remerge, plunder the loot left behind and at last inherit the earth, as was their rightful inheritance.

If people were numbered among those who responded to that call, they may still be waiting—if their food supplies have held out and their ammunition is still safely stored in case it may be needed.

The Y2K computer bug turned out to be a fizzer. No planes dropped from the sky. Electric power stations didn't stop producing energy. Financial systems didn't crash. To everyone's relief, doomsday didn't arrive with the dawn of the new millennium—at least not yet.

But neither did much else of significance seem to result in keeping with the hoped-for outcomes of the San Francisco "Urgent Appeal" for prayer and fasting. In this, Christians were to ask God "to send revival to the church and spiritual awakening to our nation." History records that the time since then has been marked by emphases given to various "progressive" movements. These, having gained ever increasing influence and acceptance, have been codified into legislation in various jurisdictions.

In Biblical and historical terms, some of these might be more accurately termed as "regressive", in that they represent a return to ancient ways long since abandoned through Christianity's influence. Today, a survey of daily media postings, might lead one to conclude that Western society seems riven with violence, criminality, poverty, injustice, division, animosity, substance abuse, gender confusion and a host of other ailments. Should that be so, if fault is to be attributed, it lies less with the world and more with the church. It has been failing in its mission as it drifted into decline and influence.

Church Decline

In the UK, mathematical modelling released on May 15, 2022, showed that based on current calculations, all major denominations were trending toward extinction by 2090, unless there was some interruption in the meantime.[138]

---

138 John Hayward, *Growth, Decline and Extinction of UK Churches*. https://churchmodel.org.uk/2022/05/15/growth-decline-and-extinction-of-uk-churches/ May 15, 2022.

In Australia, the latest census data released in June 2022, indicated that for the first time in the nation's history, those who identify as Christians were in a minority. In 2011 they numbered 61% of the population. A decade later it was 44%.[139] That represented an unprecedented, staggering rate of decline in just 10 years! A journalist writing in a national newspaper accurately summed up the situation when he wrote, "This is not a gentle decline. It is a bus hurtling over a cliff... Nothing as dramatic and consequential has happened in Australian belief and outlook since 1788 (the year of the first European settlement)."[140]

The Church's fall from public esteem has been accelerated by the exposure, across many countries, of countless sex scandals committed by those to whom it was entrusted to model and maintain its highest standards—the clergy. Other sections of the church have climbed aboard society's slippery slope in a race to the bottom, by adjusting their long held theological positions to accommodate the new moralities in the cause of common catchwords of the times—tolerance and inclusiveness. This conveniently overlooks the teaching of the Bible regarding many of the new wave of acceptable behaviors. The Bible is anything but tolerant or inclusive on such matters.

Some judge that fast-declining sections of the church are apostate. Apostasy occurs when the church forsakes its historical beliefs and practices under the influences of the world. This may legitimize the call for revival. As history shows, in that event, the reverse happens. Rather than the world influencing the church, the church influences the world.

---

139 Stephen Lunn, David Tanner, Carley Douglas, *Boom! It's the march of the millennials.* The Australian, June 28, 2022, 1.
140 Greg Sheridan, *Lost In The Secular Desert.* The Weekend Australian, July 23-24, 2022, 22.

The "Urgent Appeal" was issued in America for America. Was it not widely taken up therefore, as nothing notable on a national scale seemed to happen? Perhaps because America is such a big place with many variations, something may have occurred. But it just wasn't extensive or prolonged enough to attract international attention. Whatever may be the explanation, little seemed to have changed in America or in other Western nominally Christian nations, in the decades since the commencement of the new millennium.

The most observable movements are those that are moving away from belief in God, the Bible and the Church. There has been a rapid increase in the West in the non-Christian religions of Islam, Hinduism and Buddhism. According to sundry national census results, the most rapidly increasing group regarding religion, is those identifying as "nones". These affiliated with no religion and had no religious belief. This was particularly so among Gen Y and Gen Z–the Millennials.

The San Francisco "call" was issued in the hope of another Awakening. Some of those previous Awakenings are documented in chapter one of this book. Certainly nothing like that has since taken place. So where do we go from here? Do we give up? Is the situation hopeless? Do we join our brothers and sisters who may be still up in the hills, dug in, fortified and armed against all intruders, waiting for the end?

To all of these and any similar questions, the answer needs to be a resounding "NO!" That being so, the obvious question becomes, why do we need a revival?

The State of the State

The Church in the State and state of the Church are frequently intertwined, irrespective of constitutional separation of the two in some jurisdictions.

With the value of hindsight, it's easy to discern some of the inflection points of cultural change occurring in Western democracies in recent decades. There have been accelerants that have resulted in moves away from the former moralities and practices of bygone eras that had been undergirded by Biblical principles.

World War II sent multitudes of men off to war. This necessitated women transitioning from their traditional roles to become industrial and commercial workers supporting the war effort. With the cessation of hostilities, many women, having found new careers beyond domestic responsibilities, enjoyed life and work in the wider society. Many never returned exclusively to their former roles.

The 1950s gave personal mobility through the widespread affordability of the motorcar. It was eagerly adopted as the preferred means of transport around increasingly sprawling suburbia. This freedom on wheels, plus the introduction of the contraception pill, in part enabling the sexual revolution of the 1960s.

The 1970's witnessed a redefined, more assertive form of personalized feminism.

From there, fueled by the cultural accelerants of humanism and secularism, there was no turning back. In the increasing rush toward egocentricity of the last four decades, the privilege of belonging to and serving in community, has been swept aside by an emphasis on privatized individualism and personal "rights".

Humility has been replaced by pride. It has become the signature of ethnic identity as well as the call sign for sexual and gender alternatives. By annual weeks of celebration and marches down city streets, "pride" processions have transformed that which for centuries was regarded as aberrant, into a widely accepted new norm.

The incidence of irresponsible gambling, crime, substance abuse, pornography, domestic violence, dissolution of the extended and nuclear families, has increased apace. Our radio, print, TV and social media platforms have popularized and reinforced many of these trends.

Our governments remain largely leaderless. Instead, they take their lead from the aggregation of results from frequent surveys within the electorate. Accordingly, they legislate to pacify the processioning masses, who respectively wield more political power than the subdued silent majorities. Having long abandoned any pretense of adhering to Biblical moral absolutes, dominated by the quest to retain personal political power, what else might be expected of the democratic political elite?

City sidewalks are increasingly inhabited by homeless youths fleeing dysfunctional families, or people who have lost their jobs. Even if they had one, there was the possibility that it was too poorly paid for the employee to maintain a once previously accepted standard of living. The gap ever widens between rich and poor. When a corporate CEO is paid 2500 times the base salary of other staff and no one shouts "injustice", but accepts it as normal, history indicates that revolution may be brewing unseen.

In all of this and more, we praise ourselves for our wonderful achievements. The God of our forebears is melted down to be recast into an image of ourselves, worthy of appropriate self-adulation.

The Neutered Church

In the first half of the 20th century, the church in Europe was significantly neutered by the rise of theological liberalism. However, there was still hope over in the New World. After all, America's paper currency affirmed "In God We Trust." With the passing of the decades, questions might have arisen as to which God was the nation trusting? The answer would become clearer, as the value of the paper on which that trust was declared, increasingly came to represent more power in practice than the God to whom it referred.

The rise of the televised mega church filled stadiums with the faithful who were enthralled by celebrity pastors. They mostly preached carefully crafted, usually positive versions of an undemanding gospel. These choreographed events, enjoyed by many, masked harsher realities. The church throughout the West, was dying.

Love Redefined

Rather than biblically based beliefs defining behaviors, behaviors redefined beliefs. "Love" was paraded as the panacea for all that ailed society. Those Messianic messengers of pop culture, the Beatles, in June 1967 had declared, *All You Need Is Love*. Surely this was the way to go. After all, on their own admission, they claimed to be more popular than Jesus Christ.

So "love", that secret yearning of the human heart that finds fulfillment in acceptance by and approval of the other; "love" the most frequently flashed word on signs waved aloft by millions of street protestors; "love" the throbbing heart of countless songs endlessly recycled through media platforms; "love" that explained and excused every form of human attachment and behavior—having been hijacked from Christianity, stripped, recycled and rereleased to mean whatever anyone wanted it to mean, was recommissioned as the bright bauble of pseudo personal truth. This would guide all starry-eyed devotees to their personal nirvana, as they meditated on the summit of self-realization.

"You want to divorce your spouse, which God hates (Malachi 2:16) to remarry someone else, which Jesus called adultery apart from exceptional cases (Matthew 5:32)? No problem—so long as you love each other."

"You want to adopt any of the lifestyle practices of the Alphabet communities? Sure, if you love each other." The Apostle Paul would seriously beg to differ (Romans 1:18-32).

To even question such practices, resulted in hostile accusations with the questioner being labelled a bigot, judgmental, legalist or any number of other pejorative names. It was pointless to ask what is meant by "love". Hollywood (USA), Bollywood (India), Nollywood (Nigeria), Kollywood (Kenya) and Pollywood (Philippines), had already consistently staked out the territory as to what it should mean.

> "Love" as the Bible defines it, is bound by limits.

As the culture wars of the 2020's gained pace, other traditional Christian and Biblical beliefs were recast as hostile, hurtful or bigoted. Regarded as being at variance with contemporary mores, they were to be disallowed. To hold these values could even imperil one's livelihood and employment.

But In the Bible

The Bible sucks the oxygen from all highly charged, secular, emotional explanations. It defines the original concept that explained the timeless drama of God's interaction with humanity. "God is love" (1 John 4:8, 16). It is fundamental to God's unique character. It's what makes the God of the Bible different from every other claimant to divinity. Under these circumstances the Bible should at least be allowed to be heard.

The Bible goes further and makes explicit what is meant by "love".

"… this is love: that we walk in obedience to (God's) commands" (2 John 6).

So, "love" as the Bible defines it, is bound by limits. Love without law becomes license, that on occasion is more specifically described as lust. And this, from a Biblical perspective, is where the world has landed in its protestations of "love".

The problem is that this understanding has infiltrated the thinking of significant sections of the Western church. This in turn has birthed various practices that otherwise would have been unthinkable for most of the last two millennia.

Unsurprisingly, it is these sections of the church that are in most rapid decline. When those outside the church discern little or no difference between their behavior and the behavior of those within the church, there is nothing to attract them toward the church. Why bother? This saddened state was noted in the San Francisco "call".

Sad But Predictable

None of these things regarding the state of the church or the world should evoke surprise. Jesus said that as the end of the world approaches, there would be an increase of lawlessness and the (Biblical) love of many will grow cold (Matthew 24:12).

The Apostle Paul also foretold of an acceleration of apostasy in the same era to which Jesus referred. Former believers will fall away from the faith that had been handed down to us from our forebears (1 Thessalonians 2:1-3; 1 Timothy 4:1). As for the world, there would be a steady decline of morality in society as God gave it over to increasing debauchery and destruction (Romans 1:18-32).

In the West at least, compared to all other organizations, it may be that the church with its accumulated wealth, resources and highly trained, skilled professional staff, is the least effective in achieving its goals. The primary purpose for its existence—making disciples of all nations—is not top of its agenda.

In Australia in 2022, two of the largest denominations in the nation held national legislative councils. The headlined report from one, indicated that it was wrestling with the implications of the changing nature of same sex recognition. The other reported it was struggling with the place of women within its hierarchical structures. In both cases, no substantive agreement could be reached because of disagreements and divisions among those appointed to lead.

> **Does the church need revival? Without any doubt, the answer must be a resounding "YES"!**

Discussion of their well-documented decline hardly rated a mention. One of these denominations reportedly lost 600,000 members in the period 2016–2021.[141] Focused upon its own internal issues, the Western church failed to notice the world had moved on, to leave it sidelined, undisturbed in its determined deathly demise.

If it is asserted that the world beyond the church is in a sad and sorry state, that is not something to be sheeted home as the fault of the world. From ancient times God held His people accountable for the situation in the nation. It would only be when they humbled themselves, repented, prayed and returned whole heartedly to Him, that He would act to effect beneficial change (2 Chronicles 7:14).

The contemporary scene may result more from the state of the church that was meant to be salt and light in the world (Matthew 5:13-16) but largely isn't. If this is so, to regain its saltiness and light shining capacity, does the church need revival? Without any doubt, the answer must be a resounding "YES"!

---

141   Stephen Rice and Nicholas Jensen, *Anglicans condemn rebel 'cult'*. The Australian, August 22,2022, 5.

Does it want it? Probably not. Having been willing to live without it for so long, why should it be suddenly desirable now? Revival might be likened to a wildfire. Many would be afraid of an out-of-control spiritual fire. But we should be even more afraid of no fire at all. And dare we hope, that just as God has often responded in the past to the pleas of His people, He will intervene again to revive His church to complete His mission in the world?

Chapter 12
PRELUDE TO GLORY

Revival is the Church being what it ought to be.

Barry Chant (1938–)

Revival and Change

Revival suggests the possibility of change from imminent death to vibrant life. But in the church environment, any suggestion of change is often captured and converted into liturgy. This is a frozen zone of church inactivity. We hold to our traditions more tightly than the mandarins of government bureaucracies protect their unexamined practices.

In 1776, Catherine the Great of Russia was walking in her palace grounds. She noticed the first flower of spring in full bloom. So that it would not be trampled underfoot accidentally, she ordered a sentry to be posted to guard it. In 1903, Czar Nicholas II of Russia, walking in the same gardens, noticed a sentry standing on the same spot indicated by Czarina Catherine. The flower had long since ceased to exist, but, by imperial order, the unexamined practice had continued for 127 years!

In 1803, the British civil service posted a man with a telescope and a bell to stand on the cliffs of Dover. His duty was to watch and warn should any ships of Napoleon Bonaparte approach their Majesty's Britannic shores. Satisfied that such threat no longer existed, the position was finally abolished in

1945.[142] Although Adolf Hitler's Luftwaffe had often threatened overhead, it was reassuring to know that on the sea below, none of Napoleon's naval fleet had sailed into sight in 142 years!

> **Evangelism is humans working on God's behalf.**
>
> **Revival is God working on our behalf.**

Church and State, despite democratic legislators' best efforts to maintain their separation, continue to share at least one thing in common. Change is acceptable—only if at glacial pre-global warming speeds.

However, the San Francisco "call" regarded the matter as urgent. It cannot wait. Given the condition of the world and the church, something needs to happen—now, not later!

The well-crafted document calls for revival. But what is meant by revival?

What Is Revival

In a 1986 interview, historian of Revivals, J. Edwin Orr, explained the term's use especially in America, as follows:

> A sign in San Fernando Valley announced, "Revival every Monday!" Five miles away, in Burbank, another sign proclaimed, "Revival every night except Monday." A Texan pastor said, "We had a revival here last fall, and nobody got revived!"
>
> This understanding of "revival" is probably unique to America. It refers to evangelistic meetings and not to the more widely accepted understanding of the term.

---

142   William L. Poteet, *Have You Ever Seen a Real Revival Fire*. Ministries Today, Jan/Feb 1988, 68.

Evangelism is humans working on God's behalf. Revival is God working on our behalf.[143]

The San Francisco "call" takes 8 pages to try to define what is meant by "revival". In a 335-page book devoted exclusively to the subject of Revival, Dr Barry Chant uses 65 pages to attempt to define what is meant by the term. He concludes, "Revival is the Church being what it ought to be."[144] Attempts to agree on a concise definition of what is meant by revival, would seem to have as much hope of success as David feeling comfortable in Saul's armor.

Old Testament Renewal

Throughout the Old Testament there is the theme of recovery of apostate people. No sooner were God's people back in a healthy relationship with Him, than spiritual entropy recommenced. From experience, the end was clearly predictable.

That national cycle might be better termed renewal rather than revival. Its nadir was national depression, caused by domestic internal factors or external pressures such as military and political oppression through foreign aggression.

At the critical time, a consecrated servant of God appeared, proclaiming God's Word with power. Leaders and people being convicted of sin repented. They determined to obey God's laws. The outcome of this was all idols were destroyed, high places were torn down and worship of God in purer forms was restored. This was followed by a period of joy, gladness and national prosperity—until the next time of falling away.

Fragments of this process are seen in the episodes of repentance, reconsecration and renewal in the events surrounding:

---

143   J. Edwin Orr, recorded interview at the Congress of Itinerant Evangelists, Amsterdam, 1986.

144   Barry Chant, *This is Revival*. Adelaide, Tabor, 2013, 82.

- Joash (2 Kings 11-12)
- Asa (2 Chronicles 15:1-15)
- Hezekiah (2 Chronicles 29-31)
- Josiah (2 Chronicles 34-35)
- Haggai, Zechariah and Zerubbabel (Ezra 5-6)
- Ezra and Nehemiah (Nehemiah 8-12).

The yearning for a restoration of what had been abandoned and lost, was hauntingly expressed by Psalmists and prophets. "Will You not revive us again that Your people may rejoice in You?" (Psalm 85:6).

Their prayer acknowledged, that the initiative for these outcomes always remains with God.

That which is implicit in the Old Testament is made explicit in the New Testament, namely, the person and power of the Holy Spirit. In the Old Testament, the Spirit's anointing was for chosen persons performing special tasks; for example, for Samson to defeat Philistine oppression (Judges 14:6; 15:14) and for David to rule as king (1 Samuel 16:13).

Joel foresaw an era when the same Spirit would be available to all. "And afterward, I will pour out My Spirit on all people" (Joel: 2:28).

Jesus gave teaching about the Spirit's role and ministry (John 14:15-26; 16:5-15). Following His resurrection, Jesus explicitly promised the anointing of the Spirit for which His disciples were to wait in Jerusalem (Acts 1:8). This initiating event occurred (Acts 2:1-13). Peter interpreted it as fulfilling the prophecy spoken of in Joel (Acts 2:14-21). The elements of that event, the impact upon believers and the reaction of unbelievers, have been repeated in revivals in recent centuries during which more careful observations were made and preserved for history.

In the original Pentecostal event, the elements included:
- The blowing of a violent wind (Acts 2:2).
- What seemed like tongues of fire…that came to rest on each of the community of believers (Acts 2:3).

The immediate impact upon believers was:
- All…began to speak in other tongues (Acts 2:4).

The reactions of unbelieving observers were:
- (They) made fun of them and said, "They have had too much wine" (Acts 2:13).

Such a heightened state of spiritual activity can scarcely be maintained within normal human experience. Thus, with the passage of time, as the next generation examines the testimonies of their forebears, inevitably that which was of inexplicable supernatural origin, is reduced to an aberrant smudge across human reason. Unable to delete the recorded events of what happened, Pentecost limps into history as a topic of ideological enquiry for the quixotically curious.

The remnants of the original powerful impact may still be liturgically practiced, as in an episcopal laying on of hands in the confirmation ceremony. This is a symbolic conferring of the same Holy Spirit upon the supplicant, but mostly without any accompanying power encounter.

In our endless discussions of these matters, we have become like the Egyptians confronting Moses in Exodus 7-8. Paul would categorize them and many of us as, "always learning but never able to acknowledge the truth" (2 Timothy 3:7).

We read the testimony of Paul and others, that his preaching was, "not with wise or persuasive words, but with a demonstration of the Spirit's power" (1 Corinthians 2:4). He further claimed that "the Kingdom of God is not a matter of talk but of power" (1 Corinthians 4:20). Over 100 times, from Acts to Revelation, there are references to "power". But today, for much of the church of the West, we are of those "having a form of godliness but denying its power" (2 Timothy 3:5).

Like those original observers at Pentecost, we are more interested in critically analyzing manifestations than acknowledging transformation in lives touched by the revival Spirit. To maintain predictable order, we would much prefer that at Pentecost, the Spirit would have manifested as a gentle soothing breeze, than as a mighty rushing wind. We prefer the orderliness of the cemetery to the messiness of a nursery where new life is birthed.

There are many accounts of genuine national revivals in the last few centuries (see Chapter 1). But what might one look like closer to our time?

A Contemporary Revival

On June 18, 1995, Pastor John Kilpatrick aged 46, felt physically and emotionally weary having just lost his mother to cancer. He asked his long-time friend Stephen Hill, an evangelist, if he would preach instead of Kilpatrick. The location was Brownsville Assembly of God church in Pensacola, Florida, USA. Hill preached.

In the normal practice of an evangelist, at the conclusion of the message, Hill made a call, inviting any who wanted to receive Jesus to come to the front of the 2,800 seat auditorium. There they would be prayed for and counselled. What happened next took everybody by surprise. More than 1,000 people streamed forward in response to the preacher's invitation.

Pastor Hill felt a strong wind blowing through the building. When he prayed for a seeker, the man fell to the floor. Some people began to weep while others began involuntarily to shake violently. Evangelist Hill prayed for Pastor Kilpatrick. The Pastor fell to the floor and remained there for almost four hours. Hill later testified, that during this time he felt what he described as a heavenly glory resting upon him like a heavy blanket during which God's presence was tangible.

Having seen 1,000 people converted in one week, Hill explained the results of so many changed lives accompanied by unusual phenomena, as God's work. When God comes and takes over, all other agendas are on hold.

As the meetings continued nightly, month after month, people having heard what was happening came from ever increasing distances within and beyond the United States. Sixteen months after the commencement of the unusual phenomena in Pensacola, Eric Smith, youth pastor of First Assembly of God church in Muskogee, Oklahoma, took some of his young people to the meetings.

He testified that after attending the Pensacola meetings for three nights, he and his wife, plus several of his young people, encountered God in a new way. What he hadn't anticipated was the surprise awaiting them after returning to their home church.

As a time of praise and worship commenced in the sanctuary, youth rushed to the front of the auditorium. When the Pastor felt compelled to give an altar call during the worship time, others came to the front of the church. Soon, sounds of sobbing reverberated throughout the building as people were confessing their sins and repenting.

Teenagers collapsed on to the floor and commenced to shake as God's power touched them. The pastor also collapsed, out flat on the floor. Other teenagers went to the microphone, weeping as they confessed their sin. Young people who outwardly looked as if their Christian lives were orthodox and in good order, confessed to involvement with marijuana, hard drugs and rebellious attitudes.

The Sunday morning service continued uninterrupted into the evening service. When a 30-gallon drum was placed onto the platform, it was quickly filled with CDs, tapes, drugs, drug paraphernalia, pornography, credit cards, clothing, books, magazines, cigarettes, a Ouija board, a crack pipe and more. The church service was held for eight days in a row. The trash can was filled more than 20 times.

The apparent move of God was not confined to the church precincts. Large numbers of youth left the Sunday night meeting shaking under the power of God. That phenomenon remained with them when they attended their local public high school. The school counsellor asked Youth Pastor Smith to come to the school. A classroom was made available to him. The young people from the church and their friends were invited to attend, so that the pastor could explain what was happening.

As the pastor opened his Bible to speak, a young lady fell to her knees and delivered a powerful prophecy. It spoke of the need to get into a right relationship with Jesus. When the pastor invited a response to the prophecy, 119 students stood and began to weep. Other pastors went to other schools on similar assignments.

Back at the church several hundred people confessed faith in Jesus. Of the youth, about 300 were baptized. The movement continued.

The phenomena in this contemporary Western example—as well as many more—occur again and again in revivals whenever and wherever they happen. Whether that's in Riberalta in the Amazon Basin in Bolivia, in the 1980's[145] or in Bario, Sarawak, East Malaysia in 1973,[146] unusual phenomena were present.

---

145   Julia Love, *Real Missionaries Today*. Self-Published, 1999, 21–23.
146   Solomon Bulan and Lillian Bulan-Dorai, *The Bario Revival*. Selangor, Malaysia, Home matters Network, 2004, 7–14.

In a repeat of what began in Jesus' time and has been an element in the record of most revivals, the religious people were critical of what was happening. In the Muskogee event, on the youth scene, those who had before talked most about winning the school

Prayer is the key which unlocks the vaults of heaven.

for Jesus, chose not to participate. They maintained their attitude even as former atheists were bowing the knee and submitting to the Lordship of Jesus. Once again, God was using inexplicable phenomena that offended their minds to expose their hearts.

They became like King David's wife Michal, who, when she saw the King dancing and celebrating before the Lord as the Ark was brought into Jerusalem, she despised him. She saw only his outward activity rather than the condition of his heart. Armchair critics who prefer to watch revival from safe sideline seats, usually prefer to argue over the authenticity of physical manifestations. For them, these usually assume more importance than the evidence of supernaturally transformed lives.

Although the Brownsville event that touched many other churches did not result in a national awakening, it contained elements common to all revivals. Most noteworthily it was bookended by two common practices:

1. Prevailing prayer and
2. Negative criticism.

Prevailing Prayer

Regarding prevailing prayer, Pastor Hill and other members of the church had been praying for about three years for an empowering visitation of God's Spirit. From Pentecost in Acts 2 to the present, there is seldom a record of a prayerless revival. Prayer is the key which unlocks the vaults of heaven.

Luke 11 is the record of Jesus teaching His disciples about prayer. In verses 2-5 in response to their request, Jesus gave them a model prayer which is commonly repeated till this day. After this, He immediately then told them a story (vs 5-9) to illustrate how God responds to relentless prayer.

In the story, a man requesting bread is a friend of the one who has a capacity to grant the request. Likewise, we too are friends of Jesus, if we are numbered among His obedient disciples (John 15:14). He has the capacity to grant our request (Luke 11:9).

Note that the man is not asking anything for himself. He needs the bread to feed his guest. The Church exists uniquely for those who are not yet of its membership. Revival, while initially affecting the church, has a much wider impact on those who up to that time may never have darkened its doorstep.

Also, the hour was very late and therefore there was no other available option for obtaining food for the guest.

As we observe the situation in the world today, it appears that all the signs which Jesus said would appear before His return, are now fulfilled—with one exception. Jesus said, "This gospel of the Kingdom will be preached in the whole world as a testimony to all nations, and then the end will come" (Matthew 24:14). "To all nations" is the same as what Jesus said in the Great Commission of Matthew 28:19. There, He said that disciples are to be made "of all nations". Reaching the world's least, last and lost of previously Unreached People's Groups (UPGs), or "nations", is within reach in this generation.

Figuratively, the time may be 12 minutes to midnight and there is no other option. The message of salvation is a treasure available exclusively through disciples of Jesus—the Church.

In Jesus' story, while the door of the friend's house is obviously shut, in response to persistent knocking (v.10), it will be opened. The man persisted in his entreaties till his friend got out of bed, granted his request and handed over some bread (v.8). Finally, Jesus reassured His disciples that should we persist in prayer (vs 9–10), our Heavenly Father will certainly give that which is in our best interest, namely a visitation of the Holy Spirit (v. 13).

Such visitations are in response to extraordinary prayer, which is often led by an individual who gathers other people and encourages them to persist in prayer. When revival suddenly happens, it will be accompanied by unusual physical phenomena which will attract the criticism of non-participants.

Negative Criticism

Regarding negative criticism, of course discernment and a modicum of wise control is necessary in any move of spiritual response in the Christian community. This avoids unseemly excesses that may breach the normal bounds of accepted propriety. But that same criticism, unless checked, may also cause a cessation of the Spirit's move among God's people.

Those believers at Pentecost were accused of being drunk. In their inebriated state, drunk people are seldom too much of a danger to themselves or others, unless driving a vehicle! They are mostly happy, exuberant, exhilarated and a bit noisy. Any church gathering is usually characterized by dignity, respectability, sophistication and sobriety. In that this has seldom impacted the unchurched, perhaps a little Holy Spirit intoxication could be a good thing.

A Korean proverb states, "He that is born in the fire will not faint in the sun."

In revivals, should there be criticism or even persecution, we can still trust God to be working for our own good (Romans

8:28; James 1:2-4). He who brought Shadrach, Meshach and Abednego safely through their experience of the fiery furnace, is more than able to look after all of us during any fiery visitation of the Holy Spirit on us. The same applies no matter how intense negative criticism may become.

For much of our past, over the last century, the church of the West in relationship to the society in which it comfortably reclines, has opted not to rock the boat. We have been pleasant to all. We have mostly not wanted to ruffle any feathers by disagreeing with presidents, politicians or parliaments. We have dug our grave and society at large will happily lower us into it.

English poet, G.K. Chesterton is credited with saying: "At least five times Christianity gave all appearance of dying, having gone to the dogs. But in each case, it was the dog that died."

Today the Church is between a rock and a hard place. Unless there is change our future is not bright. Like the church in Ephesus, many in today's church have worked hard, persevered, insisted on correct doctrine, endured hardship, "and have not grown weary" (Revelation 2:2-3). Our diligence has resulted in our loving the work of the Lord more than the Lord of the work. We too "have therefore forsaken our first love" (Revelation 2:4). As it was for the Ephesians, so it is for the Church in every century. We "need to remember the height from which (we) have fallen" (Revelation 2:5). Our next step is to repent and seek the Lord.

> Our diligence has resulted in our loving the work of the Lord more than the Lord of the work.

It is not a question of God's ability or desire to reheat the dying embers of His fast-fading church. The question is, do we want Him to do so? A journalist writing for his news service, expressed it thus:

> Christians, we have to make a choice: continue on our present trajectory of self-absorbed arrogance confined to our self-contained little worlds and reap the inevitable consequences; or humble ourselves, ask for revival and 'strengthen what remains' so that we can be the blessing we were made to be.[147]

If the Lord should so favor us by sending revival, the following may help us to survive and thrive in what could be glorious chaos and deliver us even stronger for whatever is beyond.

To prepare

- Always be ready to acknowledge spiritual poverty and need of refreshment and renewal by God.
- Be open to receive humbly whatever blessing God gives in whatever form He chooses.
- Anticipate that when God moves among His people, initially it is often misunderstood because it is a messy mix of spirit and flesh.

Avoid

- Spiritual elitism if God has blessed you.
- Spiritual consumerism or spiritual tourism. Remain committed to your "home base".
- Giving too much importance to visible manifestations. They are not the best guide for the inner workings of the Holy Spirit.
- Judging other groups or individuals without first searching your own heart (Luke 6:39–44; 9:49–50).

---

147 Dan Wooding, *Chinese Christians Are Praying that Persecution Comes To The American Church So It Can Experience The Revival That Is Sweeping China.* www. assistnews.net, August 15, 2005. (Viewed August 29, 2005.)

- Being disrespectful of the integrity of others' claims and expectations (Romans 14:19).
- Anything which causes division (Ephesians 4:3; Colossians 3:12-14).

If this is a "time of refreshing from the Lord" (Acts 3:19) which is a prelude to a greater outpouring of the Spirit–

Expect To See
- Repentance and reconciliation–a spiritual clean-up operation wherever needed.
- A new hunger for God and His word.
- A heightened concern for the total condition of others.
- The lapsed being restored and conversions taking place.

At All Times Ask
- Is Jesus being glorified as Lord of all? (Colossians 1:15-20; John 16:14).
- Is there evidence of significant lasting spiritual fruit in lives being changed with time (John 15:1-8; Ephesians 5:9; Galatians 5:22-23).

During the toughest times, God challenged a despairing Ezekiel with a vital question. Having transported the prophet to a valley of dry bones, God asked, "Son of man, can these bones live?" (Ezekiel 37:3). Ezekiel gave a safe, agnostic, noncommittal answer. "O, Sovereign Lord, You alone know" (Ezekiel 37:3).

God then challenged Ezekiel with a proposition. If Ezekiel would exercise faith and do his part by telling the bones to live, God would do His part by rebuilding bodies onto the bones and causing them all to come to life again.

At the risk of being made to look a fool, Ezekiel obeyed and God did the rest.

The God we serve brings life out of death. He is all-powerful, all-knowing and ever present. He is sovereign over all. He chooses that we should cooperate with Him to fulfill His purposes. For revival our part is to pray. Prayer is the point at which the sovereignty of God meets the responsibility of humankind. We become the conduits of His glory that attracts others to enquire what these things mean.

That being so, here at the end, we return to the beginning and once more say, "Lord, teach us to pray" (Luke 11:1). As noted in chapter one, in response to the pleading of His people, again and again God responded to the prayers of His people. We have every reason to hope that as we humble ourselves and commit to pray, He will again visit us to do what only He can do (2 Chronicles 7:14).

Remember—God doesn't expect the impossible from us. He wants us to expect the impossible from Him.

And

"May the God of hope fill you with all joy and peace as you trust Him, so that you may overflow with hope by the power of the Holy Spirit" (Romans 15:13).

BIBLIOGRAPHY

Books

Bright, Bill, *The Coming Revival*. Campus Crusade for Christ, Orlando, Florida, 1995.

Bryant, David, *Concerts of Prayer*. Ventura, California, Regal Books, 1984.

Bulan, Solomon, and Bulan-Dorai, *The Bario Revival*. Selangor, Malaysia, Home Matters Network, 2004.

Chant, Barry, *This is Revival*. Adelaide, South Australia, Tabor, 2013.

Cho, Paul Y., *Prayer: Key to Revival*. Herts, England, Word Publishing, 1985.

Christenson, Evelyn, *What Happens When Women Pray*. Wheaton, Illinois, Victor Books, 1975.

Cox, F.A., *History of the Baptist Mission, Vol.1*. London, T. Ward & Co. and G & J Dyer, 1784 Circular letter of the Northampton (Baptist) Association, 1842.

Cymbala, Jim, *Fresh Wind, Fresh Fire*. Grand Rapids, Michigan, Zondervan, 1977.

Duewel, Wesley L., *Touch the World Through Prayer*. Grand Rapids, Michigan, Francis Ashbury Press, 1986.

Eastman, Dick, *No Easy Road*. Grand Rapids, Michigan, Baker Book House, 1971.

El-Masri, Inis, *The Story of the Coptic Church*. Part 3.

Farah, Warrick, Ed., *Motus Dei, The Movement of God to Disciple the Nations*. Littleton, Co., USA, William Carey Publishing, 2021.

Foster, Richard J., *Celebration of Discipline*. New York, Harper and Row, 1978.

Fraser, J.O., *The Prayer of Faith*. Sevenoaks, UK, Overseas Missionary Fellowship, 1958.

Gibson, Ian, *Suffering and Hope: Christianity and Ethics Among the Newars of Bhaktapur*. Kathmandu, Ekta, 2017.

Gonzalez, Justo L, *The Story of Christianity, Vol.2: The Reformation to the Present Day*. Grand Rapids, MI, Zondervan, 2010.

Graham, Jim. *Prayer*. London, Scripture Union, 1985.

Grubb, Norman, *Rees Howells Intercessor*. London, Lutterworth Press, 1962.

Hamilton, Scott, *Christianity in its Global Context, 1970–2020: Society, Religion and Mission*. South Hamilton, MA, Center for the Study for Global Christianity.

Hyatt, Eddie L., *1726: The Year that Defined America*. Grapevine, Texas, Hyatt International Ministries, 2019.

Kehrberg, Norma., *The Cross in the Land of the Khukuri*. Kathmandu, Elka Books, 2000.

Lawrence, Carl, *The Coming Influence of China*. Gresham, OR, USA, Vision House Publishing, 1996.

Lindsell, Harold, *An Evangelical Theology of Missions*. Grand Rapids, Michigan, Zondervan, 1970.

Long, Egerton C., *Prayer what's it all about*. Glenhaven, NSW, Australia, 1984.

Love, Julia, *Real Missionaries Today*. Self-Published, 1999.

Mahlburg, Kurt, Marsh, Warwick, *Power of Prayer*. Unanderra, NSW, Australian Heart Publishing, 2021, 107.

McKenna, Briege, *Miracles Do Happen*. London, Pan Books, 1987.

Miller, R. Edward, *Thy God Reigneth—The Story of Revival in Argentina*. Burbank, California, World Missionary Assistance Plan, 1964.

Mumford, Bob, Edythe Draper, editor, *Quotations for the Christian World*. Wheaton, Illinois, Tyndale House, 1992.

Open Doors, *Cuba for Christ*. Tonbridge, UK, Sovereign World, 1999.

Peters, George W., *A Theology of Church Growth*. Grand Rapids, MI, Zondervan, 1981.

Power, Bernie, *Jesus and Muhammad*. Moreland, Australia, Acorn Press, 2016.

Prince, Derek, *Secrets of a Prayer Warrior*. Grand Rapids, Michigan, Chosen, 2009.

Qureshi, Nabeel, *Seeking Allah, Finding Jesus*. Grand Rapids, Michigan, Zondervan, 2014.

Robinson, Stuart, *Daring to Disciple*. Upper Mt Gravatt, Brisbane, CHI Books, 2020.

Rockness, Miriam Huffman, *A Passion for the Impossible—the Life of Lilias Trotter*. Grand Rapids Michigan, Discovery House Publishers, 2003.

Tadras, Samuel, *Motherland Lost, The Egyptian and Coptic Quest for Modernity Vol. 638*. Stanford, CA, Hoover press, 2013.

The Biography of Saint Samaan the Shoemaker "The Tanner". Cairo, The Church of Saint Samaan the Tanner in Mokattam, 1998.

Torrey, R.A., *The Power of Prayer*. Grand Rapids, Michigan, Zondervan, 1974.

Wells, Tom, *A Vision for Missions*. Carlisle, Pennsylvania, Banner of Truth, 1985.

Wiersbe, Warren, *Confident Living*. Good News Broadcasting Association Inc., 1998.

Willhite, Bob, *Why Pray?* Altamonte Springs, Florida, Creation House, 1988.

Woodbridge, John ed., *More Than Conquerors*. Chicago, Illinois, Moody Press, 1992.

Yeager, Jonathan, *The Letters of Jonathan Erskine to the Rylands*. Eusebia, Spring, 2008.

Articles

Allen, R. Earl, *Quotable*. Ministries Today, July/August 1997.

Bush, Luis, *Reaching every people group in Nepal for Christ*. MARC Newsletter No. 96-1, March 1996.

Circular letter of the Northampton (Baptist) Association, 1784.

Compass Direct editors, *China: the daft, the daring and the dark*. Momentum, September/October 2005.

Corbett, Jen and McGuiness, Jan, *A consumer's guide to Hell*. The Bulletin, May 24, 1988.

Cox, Lynn, *Prayers God Cannot Answer*. On Being, August 1992.

De Arango, Gisella Guth, Joel News International 792, October 6, 2011.

Dixon, Larry, *Whatever Happened to Hell?* Moody, June 1993, 26.

Faith Tragedy in Bangladesh', Al-muslimoon Weekly, January 9 1994.

Gordon-Conwell Theological Seminary, *Christianity in its Global Context, 1970-2020: Society, religion and Mission*. South Hamilton, MA, Center for the Study of Global Christianity, 38, (viewed January 27, 2019).

God's intervention saves 72 captive Nigerian Christians from Boko Haram firing squad. Barnabas Aid, May/June 2019.

Hastings, Holly, *The Road to Community Transformation*. World InSight, Lynnwood, WA, USA, Sentinel Group, February 2000.

'If only My People will Pray', Revival World Report, September–October 2000, 18.

Kim, Joon Gon, *Prayer and Spiritual Explosion*. World Evangelization, n.d.

LeSourd, Leonard, *Stand in the Gap for Your Children*. The Intercessors, Vol.4 No. 8, Breakthrough Inc., Lincoln, VA, December 1984.

Mahaney, Charles. *Why don't I pray more?* Pastoral Renewal, April 1986.

Miller, Duane Alexander and Johnston, Patrick, *Believers in Christ from a Muslim Background: A Global Census*. Interdisciplinary Journal of Research on Religion, Vol. II, Article 10, 2015.

O'Connor, Greg, *Miracles in Cuba*. New Day, May 1990.

Olsen, Ted, *Miracles show readiness for "Table 71" in India*. Dawn Report, Issue No. 47, June 2002.

Olsen, Ted, *The story of DAWN is the saga of the exploding Church*. Dawn Around the World, Issue 2, Vol.1, November 2005.

Orpin, Grahame, *World Outreach*. January 6, 2004.

Orr, J. Edwin, Interview at Congress of Itinerant Evangelists, Amsterdam, Netherlands, 1986.

Packer, Kerry, *On God*. The Australian, February 17, 1995.

Perkins Jr., Raymond C., Prayer for Israel, New Zealand, Number 71, July–August 1993.

Praying Things Through Before They Happen. Australia, Derek Prince Ministries, December 19, 2012.

Religious Survey-7, 90-96AD Narsingdi Zone-9, Islamic Missionary Counsel of Bangladesh, 2.

Rice, Stephen and Jensen, Nicholas, *Anglicans condemn rebel 'cult'*. The Australian, August 22,2022, 5.

Robinson, Stuart, *Spiritual Warfare-Prayer*. Blackburn Baptist Church Bulletin, October 25, 1987.

Robinson, Stuart, *Prayer*. Blackburn Baptist Church Bulletin, October 23, 1988.

Salcedo, Berna, *Explosive growth in Brazil will make 250000 churches a reality*. Dawn Ministries, Issue 2 Vo.1, November 2005.

Shelley, Marshall and Susan, *When the soul cries out*. Moody, March/April 2002.

Sheridan, Greg, *Lost In The Secular Desert*. The Weekend Australian, July 23–24, 2022.

Something Beautiful for God. Time, September 15, 1997.

Webb, Allan, *Fast and Pray*. East Asian's Millions, Vol.105, No.3 1997.

Webb, Allan, *Unleashing the Power of Prayer*. East Asia's Millions, Vol.104, No.2.

When prayer walking is an essential component of church planting. Dawn Around the World, Dawn Ministries, Issue 2 Vol.1, November 2005.

Wilkinson, R., *Unanswered Prayer—A Trial of Faith*. New Life, March 11, 1993.

Woodward, Kenneth L. *Is God Listening?* Newsweek, April 1, 1997.

World Revival News, Revival World Report. July/August 1999.

Yaxley, Trevor, *William and Catherine: The Life and Legacy of the Booths*. Ada, MI, Bethany House.

Hell 'frozen out' of preachers' sermons. Charisma News Service, June 19, 2002.

Internet

Abbot, Rebecca, *The Source of Denzel Washington's Advice to Will Smith*. https://www.eternitynews.com.au/current/the-source-of-denzel-washingtons-advice-to-will-smith/ March 29, 2022.

Anonymous, *Prepare to Fly*. http://www.mountainwings.com (viewed March 26, 2003).

Bragga, Amaury et al, Joel News Service. http://www.openheaven.com/forums/printer-friendly-posts.asp?FID=3&TID-10353, June 6, 2006 (viewed July 8, 2006).

Bright, Bill, *Mau Mau Uprising*. Daily Inspirations, July 8, 2021. https://www.crosswalk.com/devotionals/insights-from-bill-bright/mau-mau-uprising-july-8.html (viewed May 13, 2022).

Dunkirk Evacuation and *The Battle of the Bulge*, https://www.beliefnet.com/inspiration/3-times-prayer-changed-history.aspx (viewed December 27, 2021).

Gains, Adrienne, *South African Minister Credits 24-7 Prayer With 840,000 Salvations*. Worldwide Kingdom Revival NEWS. http://www.openheaven.com/forums/printer-friendly-posts.asp?FID-3&TID-32808, June 10, 2010 (viewed June 11, 2010).

Gibson, Ian, Gellner, David, Saro, Ramon. *Suffering and Christianity: conversion and ethical change among the Newars of Bhaktapur.* https://ora.ox.ac.uk/objects/uuid:3eedel-3f8e-4564-887f-17aaw26de57f, 2015 (viewed December 10, 2021).

Hale, Beth, *Police chief hails power of prayer in driving down town's crime rates.* Mail Online, https://www.dailymail.co.uk/news/article-1252708/Policeman-called-churchgoers-asking-for-prayer. February 22, 2010 (viewed February 27, 2010).

Hyatt, Eddie, *A Message for America from Her Two Greatest Presidents.* https://www.charismanews.com/culture/89296-a-message-for-america-from-her-two-greatest-presidents.

Jeter, Stan, *Christian Police Transform Community Through God.* Worldwide Kingdom/Revival NEWS. http://www.openheaven.com/forums/forum-posts-asp?TID=32756, April 6, 2010, (viewed June 11, 2010).

Lincoln, Abraham, *Proclamation 85—Proclaiming a Day of National Humiliation, Prayer and Fasting,* August 2, 1861. https://www.presidency.ucsb.edu/documents/proclamation-85-proclaiming-day-national-humiliation-prayer-and-fasting.

Lincoln, Abraham, *Proclamation 97—Appointing a Day of National Humiliation, Fasting and Prayer.* https://www.presidency.ucsb.edu/documents/proclamation-97-appointing-day-national-humiliation-fasting-and-prayer.

Müller, George, *Orphanages Built by Prayer.* https://www.christianity.com/church/church-history/church-history-for-kids/george-mueller-orphanages-built-by-prayer-11634869.html

Praying Through the Window III—The Unreached Peoples. Christian Information Network, Colorado Springs USA, http://www.christian-info.com.

OpenHeaven.com—*Cuba is seeing one of the fastest growth rates in the world.* http://www.openheaven.com/forums/

printer_friendly_posts.asp?FID=3&TID=34754, November 28, 2010.

50% dos brasileiros são católicos, 31% evangélicos e 10% nãotêm religîao, diz Datafolha, (viewed December 1, 2021).

Prayer: No. 1 issue in churches, survey of leaders shows. www. hapnews.org. April 12, 2005.

Saia, Carol, *God Ends Idol's 700-year Reign in Guatemalan Village.* Worldwide Kingdom/Revival NEWS. http://www.openheaven. com/forums/printer-friendly-posts.asp?FID=3&TID=34664, July 11, 2010 (viewed November 13, 2010).

Simon, Wolfgang, Translator Steven Bufton. Friday-Fax Issue 43, Friday-fax@bufton.net, November 4, 2005.

Warren, Rick, Pastors.com, *Encouraging pastors and church leaders with tools for healthy, growing churches.* Issue 224, September 14, 2005 (viewed January 28, 2006).

Wooding, Dan. http://assistnews.net/index.php/component/k2/item/981-how-suffering-made-cubas-churches-grow. September 12, 2015.

ABOUT THE AUTHOR

Dr Stuart Robinson is the Founding Pastor of Australia's largest Baptist Church. Before that he worked for fourteen years in South Asia where he pioneered church planting among a previously very resistant majority people group. He travels extensively as a speaker at Seminars, Conferences and Colleges. He is the author of thirteen books including best-selling titles, *Mosques & Miracles, Defying Death, The Prayer of Obedience* and *The Challenge of Islam*. He graduated from four tertiary institutions. Stuart was born in Brisbane Australia and is married to Margaret. They have three married children.

www.drstuartrobinson.com

Printed in Australia
Ingram Content Group Australia Pty Ltd
AUHW010900250624
396163AU00003B/5

9 780648 510895